THE SILVER BULLET
EASY LEARNING SYSTEM

How to Change Classrooms Fast and
Energize Student for Success

JOHN JENSEN

To order additional copies of this book, contact:
Xlibris Corporation
1-888-795-4274
www.Xlibris.com
Orders@Xlibris.com
32329

CONTENTS

ACKNOWLEDGMENTS

Many people have helped me with the ideas I report here. I'm indebted especially to Gerry Dunne, Uvaldo Palomares, and Jerry Southard who included me in the groundbreaking Human Development Program in the early 1970s. The program recognized the key role of children's affective development and showed how changes in their attitudes and personal mastery were possible faster than anyone had imagined. This realization helped start me on the thirty-six years of effort that have come together in this book.

When I had the basics of the present design in hand, Joe Drake's invitation to present it to the African American Academy staff in Seattle was a turning point. Together there, Leonard Dawson, Jr., and I worked out how to apply it daily with a difficult class. I appreciate the cooperation of principals Ora Franklin, Larry Ecklund, Charles Kaplan, Pam Slyter, Linda Bauer, Gary Emslie, Eric Bolz, and Ron Erickson for allowing me to try out ideas with teachers, and many of the latter who applied them, especially Ann Whitelaw, Heidi Bennett, Judy Hoeldt, Elaine Barbour, Marcia Strang, Judy Vavrek, Mary Champagne, Barbara Jones, Jude Edwards, and many in Haines, Alaska. Michael LaFlamme aided with his thinking about structures, Sheila and Martin Nickerson hosted the "perfect conversation," my son Solan was a willing subject for many learning experiments, and Elaine Paul offered valuable suggestions about the text. Finally, the two years of Eagle School for older students who'd given up on the public system wouldn't have been possible without the versatility and commitment of Nels Becker and Elena Del Moral. They sustained my belief that these methods could work with any students.

My thanks to you all.

INTRODUCTION

How do you nail a piece of learning?

The context is sports, as in nailing a 3-point basket, a vault dismount, or a downhill ski run. Implied are a key moment, a special effort, and a demonstration of excellence that leaves no doubt. In school, we watch a kindergarten teacher nailing learning on the first day of school:

"When you're on the playground and the bell rings, you form a line at the door. Now, what do you do when the bell rings?" They all answer together, "We form a line at the door."

The teacher congratulates them, and in a box on the board writes "1". She tells them, "You just learned one thing. Wasn't that easy? That's what we're going to do every day. We're going to learn lots of easy things and count them up. Now what was it, again, that you do when the bell rings?" They answer, "Line up at the door!"

"One more time," she says, "and louder."

"Line up at the door!" they shout.

Now they own that piece of knowledge, and proceed to rules for the classroom and onward into their lifetime of knowledge: get this point, own it, get another, own it, and so on. The score written in the box on the board is like a deed to a piece of ground, a claim that this chunk is theirs for good. Minute by minute, they nail pieces of learning and feel invigorated. Their key moment is the teacher's challenging question, their special effort is to listen, their demonstration is to answer firmly, and the result is pleasure at success.

Education always at that level, of course, would be like basketball as only a free throw contest—repeating a single behavior. The game is interesting instead because of the many ways to nail a demonstration of excellence—a tomahawk dunk, a perfectly executed fast break, an agile block, a crucial jump shot. Producing them organizes an entire field of effort and learning.

Back to the schoolroom and kindergartners grown older. How do they get the same sense of challenge, special effort, and achievement? How does nailing their learning guide their effort? That's the question I try to answer here, making learning firm enough to satisfy any test yet with the emotional flavor of a 3-point shot in the closing seconds of a basketball game.

I should point out that I'm not a teacher by trade though I've taught many courses, and not a researcher. While I appreciate good research and cite a few useful pieces, over the years I've noticed that teachers are seldom moved by it, and that the few conditions that really matter are so familiar as to be almost boring:

1. Skill development of any kind depends on practice.
2. Feelings and communications affect learning.
3. Students need to know where to place their effort.
4. They need increments of success and reinforcement for them.
5. They develop comprehensive knowledge by assimilating it piece by piece.

Nothing startling there. Some ways of doing those simple things discourage students, however, and others stimulate them by how they engage students' energy—which typically responds quickly. You don't need a district reorganization to know. In a few days you say, "This interests them. They sit up and take notice and want to keep going, and they're learning."

I've seen the ideas explained here succeed from kindergarten through high school, and with the most difficult students any teacher is likely to encounter. I worked for six months at the Lake Washington Individual Progress Center with high school students who had severe emotional and behavioral disabilities, and conducted a school in my home for two years with middle and high school students who couldn't manage the public system. I've shared the methods with teachers in Washington, Minnesota, New Mexico, and Alaska, observing their progress and learning with them, and applied the ideas to an acrimonious fourth grade that's described in detail in Chapter 9. If this sample appears too small, note the time frame I suggest. In a few days you can test the ideas with no financial outlay, no new curriculum, and no one looking over your shoulder. Use them with what you already teach, and watch students learn and feel better.

This isn't a book about school organization, charters, vouchers, leadership, labor policy, educational ideology, teacher training, or countless other legitimate concerns. Innumerable qualities individuate one school from another, and problems must be solved as they present themselves. Here we confine our focus to the ordinary tasks in one room hour by hour between teacher and students.

A clue about how to arouse energy for learning came to me in the early 1990s.

On a Saturday afternoon when my son was in middle school, I watched him and his friends dash about a rain-soaked field in a soccer game. They were motivated, yet almost all were indifferent students. I could imagine them walking into school through an invisible force field that zapped their wits.

How was the play field different from the classroom? The participants were the same, so it had to be their dynamics. On the field, twenty-two boys were motivated, executing tiring maneuvers under unpleasant conditions, but they demonstrated skill, scored to validate their effort, linked effort to results, had team support, performed publicly, and practiced to improve. A few simple guidelines unlocked the energy. Where, I wondered, was the pocket rule book that told how to do the same in classrooms?

The skill we want to reveal is the expression of learning. Imagine a student standing before his class, confident of what he knows, and enthusiastically and expertly explaining it. He practices to acquire skill, performs in public, and is acclaimed successful.

Teachers model this. What they do to teach is what students need to do in order to learn. They obtain the knowledge in print, identify what is important in it, organize it, get it in their head, and express it over and over. As it becomes familiar, it affords them pleasure and creativity. They entertain challenges to it, add to it, reflect on it, and re-organize it. Students can't do without any of those steps. They need the subject printed, prioritized, organized, impressed in mind, expressed repeatedly, added to, and modified. All the steps are critical at their right moment but they also appear to make education more complicated.

One feature of soccer, I realized, unified its tasks as it does with every sport, and simplified the classroom problem. In soccer, *the whole effort hinges around how increments of success are identified*. The soccer goal incorporates all the behaviors that lead up to it, so that players always know where to aim their effort. We look for a similar increment of effort that can organize classroom learning.

Both national legislation and common experience identify it: to be able to tell back what one has learned, usually by test-taking. Put differently, mastery is *the ability to explain something without help*. Remove help and ask a question. What students can answer is what they know, and the boring principles above tell how. Because some ways of applying them are deadening, we need to find ones instead that enable students to be and feel constantly successful.

At one level, how students learn is remarkably uniform. They take in a piece and then bring it out to demonstrate that they have it. They own that piece and then go for another. Absorbing and owning a point at a time, the first day they may have "12" in the box on the board. The next day they reclaim the prior day's work so they don't lose it, and add more. Stated in terms of their effort, their education mainly consists of accumulating pieces they can explain back. If every hour you arrange for them to increase what they can explain, they steadily expand their knowledge. Their score tells you where to direct their energy next, and they know clearly where it has gotten them—two understandings that help generate a successful class. Their increments nailed and counted this way present validly what they're aware of knowing, are measured the same by everyone, and need no comparison with other students.

Of the seven core elements of the Silver Bullet Easy Learning System, five help to master knowledge, two create a positive atmosphere, and fifty-four activities apply them.

Understand. Students understand what is conveyed or presented.

Organize. They organize it to make it easy to practice, save, and retrieve.

Practice. They assimilate knowledge by explaining and expressing it.

Score. They score their learning objectively by counting points of knowledge gained or timing their explanation.

Perform. They stand and perform what they know.

Good feelings. They give each other good feelings.

Communications. They improve the quality of their communications.

The methods aren't separated by grade level because first graders can become just as proficient at many of them as older students. Teachers will readily understand what they can adapt to their students just by practice. Overall, fresh energy steadily comes available from understanding, organizing, talking, mental review, self-rating, feedback, performing, scoring, communicating, and sharing good feelings. Rather than focusing on the stresses that make students drop out, we can make their classroom experience so successful and satisfying that their determination to remain in school outweighs other influences they put up with.

The title of the book is a response to the assertion that no single factor could turn education around quickly. To the contrary, the effort needed is commonplace, students' manner of learning isn't that different one to another no matter what their prior knowledge or disability, and the outcomes aren't hard to achieve. If we just arrange for students actually to accumulate and save knowledge hour by hour, this will shortly transform American education.

We begin in Chapter 1 with imagining a visit to a classroom that's begun to use the design. Chapters 2-8 describe the methods in detail, arranged in several categories. The first set offers nine "quick-start" methods that comprise the basic structure for success and good feelings. Chapters 3-4 show how to develop refined communications and aid students' emotional self-management. Chapters 5-8 explain how to practice learning to generate permanent retention, ways to think about designing a curriculum and focusing student effort, how scoring instead of grading can solve the problem of assessing student learning, and ways students can demonstrate their learning that stimulate them to invest greater energy in it. Chapter 9 narrates how a troubled class applied the approach, Chapter 10 treats several issues about implementation, and appendices and references conclude the book.

Depending on the context, my use of "we" may mean "you and I," "we humans," or "those who work in classrooms." When able to choose between terms in general use or those with specialized educational meaning, I try to stay with the former if their meaning is clear. I sometimes use boldface within paragraphs rather than section headings to emphasize key ideas, and also to present a teacher's words for applying a method. Sub-numbering within sections generally is to unify a set or sequence. Parenthetical numbers preceded by *cf.* refer you to one of the fifty-four methods, and my capitalization of a method within a paragraph indicates that it's explained in more detail elsewhere.

CHAPTER 1

Sample Period

U ndirected student energy faces us, and we organize it. We try to fill each moment with an activity of value. Time matters, and we use it purposefully, channeling effort. Students welcome being mobilized in an activity, and intensive discipline can be stimulating.

An illustration of this idea occurred when I was taking my turn leading my ROTC class in college. The corps had turned out for a parade, and my platoon and I were waiting in formation on a side street beforehand. Suddenly I heard a call, "Hey Lieutenant, how about some close order drill?"

I brightened, sang out "Atten-HUT!" and everyone came to attention. For several minutes within the confines of a single street and cadets on either side of us watching, I called out commands that they followed readily one after another: "Forward, *march*. To the rear, *march*. By the right flank, *march*," and so on. Everyone knew what to do. When we returned to our assigned spot, they felt refreshed, and the remaining time passed quickly.

In a typical K-12 period, little learning may engage their energy—perhaps 10-15 minutes per hour—while the rest is open to distraction or boredom. In the sample period that follows, the activities aim to engage students steadily.

Visit to a classroom. Imagine that a school recently implemented the program and a teacher invites you to observe. You enter before students arrive, and she welcomes you. "Let me show you what I'm planning," she says, and hands you the schedule:

Review practice	**5 min**
My presentation and discussion	**15 min**
Communication skills selection	**1 min**
Partner practice and scoring	**24 min**
Communication skills feedback	**2 min**
Mental movie	**3 min**
Total	**50 min**

"Explain it to me," you say.

"The heart of the hour is the fourth activity, the practice. Students explain to partners what they just learned. For about twenty minutes they express in their own words what they got from the presentation, each one using half the time, and end knowing most or all of the lesson. From then on, periodic recall makes it permanent. First thing next class, they sink it deeper by recalling it again in review practice."

"Are they learning a lot with it?"

"We're right on track. We're aiming for a minute's worth of new knowledge every class. I usually explain a section and write it on the board. They copy it and I make sure they understand it."

"I notice two activities for communication skills," you say. "How do they fit in?"

"We integrate communications with learning. Students look at a skills sheet to select a skill to use while working with their partner. Taking just a few seconds to think ahead, they're more conscious of something as simple as looking at the person who's speaking. After the practice, they get feedback from their partner, who tells them such things as 'You seemed interested in what I was saying' or noting their use of a skill. We work on communications in other ways too."

"And what's Mental Movie?"

"They close their eyes and recall everything they saw, heard, or did during the class, as though watching the raw footage of a class film. Most of them have good visual memories, so this draws the whole period together. Usually two or three minutes are enough. Sometimes we use that final time for Impromptu Performance. They stand and answer questions about what they learned."

The teacher stops speaking as students walk in, and you sit down. Students look at a partner list by the door, find the one assigned to them, and take chairs together. Several open their notebooks and begin talking at once. When the bell rings to begin the period, the teacher says, "Please review with your partner if you haven't already." All open their notebooks and one from each pair begins talking. A student near you accepts another's notebook, asks a question from it, and then scans an Answers page while listening. The speaker says, "Ask me number fourteen. I'm not sure about that one." His partner does so, and coaches briefly while the speaker summarizes. After a couple minutes, they trade notebooks and the former listener becomes speaker. They lean toward each other, intent on what they do.

Presentation. The teacher ends the review and begins a lesson about the industrial revolution: "The question we're going to deal with and copy on your Questions page is 'How did the industrial revolution affect workers?' She writes it at the top of the board and students copy it. As she speaks, she directs their attention to pictures in their text, and writes key ideas on a vertical strip next to the board titled Peg List:

craftsmen
unemployment
Ned Ludd
Luddites
Birmingham

She reads from Dickens' book *Hard Times* while students close their eyes and imagine it; then adds to the Peg List the book, author, and other ideas she presents:

Dickens
Hard Times
wages/hours
crippling
disability
overlooker
strapping

Two raise their hands with questions, and she adds other words to the Peg List as she answers.

Questions. With each word she puts on the Peg List, she writes a portion of the overall answer on the board in summary phrases and sentences while students copy them:

Before industrial rev. work done by skilled craftsmen.
Use of machines put many out of work.
Ned Ludd/ Luddites smashed machines, burned factories, punished, some hanged.
Factory towns, Birmingham, grew 4x in 50 years, many homeless
***Hard Times* images: chimneys, smoke, noise, purple water, crowds**

Partner Skills. After fifteen minutes of presentation, she says "Before you practice what we've covered, please open your notebooks to the communication skills and pick out one or two to use." Students open their notebooks, heads bob up and down briefly, and the teacher continues.

Partner Practice. "Take twelve minutes each now and tell back everything you can remember that we covered. Each should be first to try half of it. If neither of you can remember a piece, refresh your memory by glancing at it, and try it again. When your partner has a chunk mastered, time their telling of it, and in their notebook under the question, mark the time and your initials."

"Can we add other stuff we read?" a student asks.

"If you've read from other books and articles, add in what you have time for. If you want, you can take notes on what your partner says to add to your own."

Another hand goes up. "I read a lot about it last night and I don't think I can tell it all back in the time I have."

"If you've outlined the answer in the Answers section of your notes as I suggested, you'll be able to hold onto it. Tell back the outline so you have the overview well in mind. On Friday we'll have a mastery review day when you can either check the timing of pieces you've already done or add new ones, so save big chunks till then to practice. Will that work for you?"

"Sure," he says.

The students exchange notebooks. The teacher assigns the first speakers to be those having first names with the earliest letter of the alphabet, and walks slowly through the classroom listening as they set to work.

Scoring. She returns to the board and writes three reminders:

1 **Write your partner's time under the question in their notebook with your initials beside it.**

2 **Write both of your names and scores on one slip of paper to turn in.**

3 **Tell your partner what skills he or she used that seemed to help you.**

At ten minutes, she gets their attention and suggests that they switch if they haven't already. After twenty-two minutes, she calls time, points to the items on the board, and says, "Please complete your record-keeping and then do the feedback on skills." You see glances at the wall clock, and pencils moving in notebooks and on small slips of paper.

They turn their notebooks back to the skills list they looked at before practicing. The buzz of conversation resumes as they comment to each other. This is over in a minute, and the teacher says "Tomorrow we'll work on the Communication Skills Check Sheet some more and do Appreciation Time. Till then, please notice the skills you see others using.

"We have a couple minutes before the bell, so could I ask everyone to do Mental Movie for the remaining time? Sit upright and comfortable, close your eyes, and try to recapture everything you learned today. Make images out of all the ideas, hear all the sounds that accompany them, and recall your movements and feelings."

Students straighten their book bags, collect their materials, and settle in their seats. Shortly, everyone is still with eyes closed. Three minutes later when the bell rings, a few spring-loaded students are on their feet moving toward the door while others remain motionless. A minute later the last ones open their eyes, and drop their score slips into a basket on the teacher's desk as they leave.

Debrief. Alone with the teacher, you point to a posted list titled Learning Activities and ask, "Would you explain these?"

"I've already mentioned several," she says. "We display them to remind students that they can use these methods to learn on their own.

Present means to offer knowledge to someone else. That's mostly me, but students do it when they read a book and share it with someone else. With *Understand* we commit to each one understanding the first time something is presented. Sometimes their partner fills in what they didn't get from me and there are a few students I check on. In *Partner Practice* they re-tell the learning to someone else. They're also mastering nine ways to help their partner, like 'waiting while the other recalls,' 'asking partner to explain what he/she knows least,' and 'helping each other summarize answers.'

"*Questions and Answers* means organizing their notebooks that way. We separate them to different pages to make the notebook a better practice tool. *Scoring* refers to students timing or counting points of others' knowledge for a score under that question. I have their score slips now that I'll post later." She points to a large scoreboard with names on it. "The numbers," she says, "are their scores, their daily and cumulative time and points that count up what they can explain back.

"*Mental Movie* we did a minute ago. With *Perform,* I draw a question from those they've practiced and then the name of a student to answer it. Sometimes we do these two back to back.

"*CSCS* means the Communication Skills Check Sheet. I asked them to look at it and pick out skills to work on during Partner Practice. *Understanding Causality* is a class discussion applying cause and effect to a feeling so students can tell when they're starting a chain in motion. We've done this twice and students like it. *Appreciation Time* is powerful. After lunch they tell how others gave them good feelings or were helpful or friendly. It sounds simple but it meets their need to be validated and makes their behavior more positive. They already treat each other differently."

"What's changed most for you in this approach?" you ask.

"I hadn't realized how much time I waste in class and how aimless they often are. The method has given me a purpose for even one spare minute. I'm better at keeping them focused."

"And your next step?" you ask.

"I'll integrate other methods gradually," she says. "Next week we'll organize the class into small groups for more student responsibility, and I'm planning a stand-up performance for parents at the end of the month."

"Would you tell the class I'm interested in their results, and will be at their performance?" you say.

"I'd be delighted," she says, "and so will they."

CHAPTER 2

Quick Start Methods

The methods in this chapter applied together enable students K-12 to experience steady increments of success and validation. To adapt the practice mode to the youngest students, cf. 32. Primary Grades.

1. Organize Notebooks

Students' notebooks are the main tool organizing their effort. To make learning content easy to practice and absorb, we separate questions from answers like a test. Then even working alone they can read a question, recall what they can about it, and turn to answer pages to fill in the details they missed. The steps below help them set it up it for multiple subjects. If you see them only for one, just separate questions and answers to different pages:

"Open your looseleaf notebook." If they use a wire bound notebook, see section below.

"Make the first page of the notebook the table of contents." They title the first page "Table of Contents" and fill it in as they organize their notebook.

"Make a section for each subject in the order you have them through the day." Use section dividers or write the names of subjects at the top of separate pages. Title a section Miscellaneous for their learning from experiences, reading, and alternate sources.

"After each subject title, add a half dozen blank pages." See that everyone has several sheets after each subject.

"Title the first page after the divider Questions and the second, Answers." On the latter page and those after it, students write a summary of everything they learn about the subject, including references to a text or other sources.

For interest, suggest an alternate title for their Questions page. "Learning Feats" hints at preparation for public performance. If they resist writing out a separate page for questions, ask them to title it "Exam Questions."

Schedule a test for the next day, dictate questions they copy exactly, and to that list add a question for everything you want them to know for the semester. Check that their numbers for questions and answers dovetail. Ask them to print their notes to make them more legible and shareable.

If their **wire-bound notebook** is already divided into subject sections with pages that can't be shifted, title the *first* page of a section Answers. Write answers in it from the beginning toward the back as usual. Title the *last* page of the section Questions and number these pages from the back of the section toward the front. When the question and answer pages meet, start a new notebook or open a new section in that one.

2. Understand

You probably apply the following automatically. For a self-check, note how you use input and output to transmit understanding.

Input. In the physical situation, remove or settle *distractions*. If their minds are on earlier events, bring them into the present.

Focus their *attention* on what you're about to say, and ask for their eyes on you.

Speak with a *clear voice* enunciating all words.

Check everyone's *hearing.* Those in back rows may miss low-volume or quickly spoken words, and many may have hearing deficits. Find out which. Seat those with poor hearing closer to you and monitor what they pick up.

Stay with *simple,* specific words that form a mental picture.

Use *gestures,* visual aids, and diagrams as appropriate.

Proceed with explanations *step by step*, providing them an impression their short-term memory can grasp.

Write out key points on the writing board to examine part by part.

They *ask questions* as needed and shift their attention from one part to another as it stands before them on the board, in a book, in their notes, or in your words.

Forecast an occasion of its *use:* that it will be tested, explained to a partner, presented to the class, or written. They retain better what they code as autobiographical, as something about themselves: "I'm going to stand and explain this."

Output. Students form their knowledge into a model they can express. What they say assures you that they received what you sent.

Ask them to *explain back* what you said, or *ask a question* and pause before naming a student so that everyone can formulate an answer.

You may ask them to explain specific, individual points to another student for a minute to give small doses of *practice putting words* to ideas (1).

Expecting a student to explain something after rudimentary exposure to it may seem over-optimistic, yet a gradient develops. With one bit of knowledge, they repeat it. With two, they can focus on one or the other; can compare, contrast, separate, and sequence. With three, they move to whole and part, relationships, and causal links. Possibilities increase with each new point added, inviting a synthesis of how everything goes together.

Make your questions **open-ended**: "Tell us about . . ." or "Would you explain (show) how . . ."?

Monitor **changes in their energy,** their need to assimilate what you presented before, and possible distractions that may arise.

Make your instruction and directions clear:

Put away your books. You're going to take a test.

Please take out a clean sheet of paper.

Copy this down exactly.

Please close your books and stand up. We're going to do something different.

Work with your partner to develop a summary of what's on the board.

Pair up and explain this to each other. When your partner knows it, raise your hand.

For the next hour, with your partner, ask each other all the questions we've studied this last week, switching back and forth with each question.

When you both know them all, let me check you.

When you say anything, you press them to pay attention but may unwittingly leave them in confusion. Was your comment just a passing one, a housekeeping issue, or learning that appears unimportant because you leave it? What are they to do? Imagine their energy as coming to a stop. They wonder, "Do I go this way or that? What's coming next? How do I cope?"

They need a means of proceeding to their next activity by sorting through your words. They must separate what to hold onto from what to release in order to direct their effort. To apply themselves to one point and not another, they have to tell them apart. The crucial step to satisfy that need is to define *the piece that requires sustained action* in written form.

3. Hard Copy

Students depend on hard copy for much of their initial learning and fill in missing pieces by revisiting it. There are several ways to provide it:

You write it fully on the board for them to copy.
You point it out in a text.
They copy it from reference sources.
They write complete notes under your oversight.
They have a book they can keep and mark up.
You give them a detailed handout.

Your own written summary that they copy is the best because: 1) With it you can integrate threads from multiple sources. 2) You clarify the points you expect them to retain out of everything you present or guide them to find. 3) Writing paces your expectations. You'd love to deliver quantities of knowledge *globatim.* You offer a feast but must wait patiently while they chew down morsels. By writing what matters most, you discipline your expansiveness and focus their effort. 4) Having a defined, orderly form for their work increases their desire to claim it. With a hole-puncher, comb bindings, and cover stock, every year students can make a book of their concentrated learning.

Usually you determine the content, but the more mature your class, the more they can gather and summarize it for all to copy.

4. Learning Feats

Once they have a record of their learning, they can practice it to make it their own.

Our culture typically quantifies feats in order to honor a competency and distinguish it from others. Think of the quantities implied in the motto of the Olympics: *Fortius, altius, citius* (stronger, higher, faster). We apply the same kind of energy and exactness to the mastery of learning. By casting it as a visible performance after special preparation, we draw on a familiar frame of reference. A Learning Feat thus is *a chunk of learning a student can explain without help that's scored by points or time,* its content identified in hard copy. The student

masters it by Partner Practice (cf. next section) or other means
explains it to another student, a parent, or the class
is awarded its precise score (cf. Chapter 7)
claims it as part of his/her permanent learning (cf. 51. Academic Mastery Report)
can replicate it any time

For the uninvolved, the content is less important at the start than their realization that they succeed. On my first day with a severely emotionally disturbed high school boy, I let him pick what he wanted to study. Unwilling to speak a word to me, he pulled a *Far Side* cartoon book from the shelf.

Twenty minutes later, to quantify his progress, I asked him to tell me the cartoons he could remember. Without hesitating, he described seventeen in sequence from memory, a remarkable accomplishment revealing a concentrated mind that was his start into classroom cooperation.

5. Partner Practice

After students receive a chunk of knowledge and write it out as questions and answers, they pair with a partner. They hand each other their notebooks and ask and answer the questions.

As noted in Chapter 1, an hour usually begins with reclaiming prior material. Invite them to begin partner practice on their own: "When you walk in, sit down and begin your mastery review with your partner. Listeners, go over your partner's notebook and ask any previous questions to help them maintain the answers. Speakers, tell your partner which questions you need to practice, and fill in parts you're missing." When they've spent a few minutes at that, you present more knowledge (or specify how they'll find it).

Partner steps. Have them copy these steps and follow them until they know them.

Nine steps for partner practice.
1   **Identify your partner for the day.**
2   **Sit where you can hear each other while speaking softly.**
3   **Listen for the teacher's signals to begin and end the activity.**
4   **Choose who speaks first and then trade roles.**
5   **Pick the questions and communication skills you'll practice.**
6   **Listener asks the speaker questions from the speaker's list.**
7   **Speaker practices answer till ready to score it.**
8   **Listener records score under the question with his/her initials.**
9   **Listener turns in score to teacher for posting.**

Before scoring "for the record," students may take a day or more to practice an answer. The score either counts the points of knowledge in an answer or times its explanation to the second. The listener records the speaker's score in the speaker's notebook under the question. When prior material is re-scored, a new, higher count is added if the mastery level increases (or lower if it declines). By maintaining accurate scores for each question, at any time you can add up the last figure under every question back to the beginning of the term to obtain a reliable total of the student's current knowledge that you post on the room's scoreboard (cf. Chapter 7).

The number of points awarded to a question are just the number of points of knowledge in the answer that you'd credit if they appeared on a test, usually one sentence per point. Many questions may elicit discrete pieces or steps that you'd mark wrong if missing. If there are six points in an answer and the speaker tells them all, the listener jots down a 6 with his/her initials beside it in the speaker's notebook, or if just three are told back, then a 3. For examples of scoring, cf. 44 and 54.

Point out the skills you want them to use as they help each other. From the lists below, add a new item daily. Eventually, convert each list to a Learning Feat so they have clearly in mind many ways to help each other.

Nine ways to help your partner learn.
1   **Listen silently while your partner recalls everything he/she can.**
2   **Ask your partner to explain what he/she knows, from least to best.**
3   **Help improve or expand answers.**
4   **Summarize answers and write them out completely.**
5   **Correct errors.**
6   **Identify what's most important.**
7   **Offer images, analogies, and ways to remember.**
8   **Give a personal touch to the knowledge.**
9   **Combine small answers into larger ones.**

As their confidence grows, speakers can invite listeners also to ask questions in a different form, draw out ideas behind the answers, and help them re-organize the knowledge.

Ten partner communication skills.
1   **Look at the speaker.**
2   **Feel respect and consideration.**
3   **Ask questions.**
4   **Take an interest in what they say.**
5   **Remember what they say.**
6   **Use their words and ideas.**
7   **Note similarities and differences compared to your ideas.**
8   **Check out your guesses about their thoughts and feelings.**
9   **Give compliments.**
10 **Tell what helped you.**

Pair with everyone. Assign new practice partners when you want to broaden connections and reinforce interest in prior material. Facing a new person is a new occasion for demonstrating competence. To the same person our presentation may seem unneeded. We already showed this person that we know it. A new face invites recasting the material, employing social skills, and keeping the knowledge fresh.

If your class has stable numbers and you'd like to partner everyone systematically, list them all in a column with names evenly spaced apart. Crop the column into a long strip with no margins at the top or bottom.

Form it into a loop, and tape the bottom and top together like a bracelet with the names around the outside.

To match names, crease the bracelet between two names, smooth it out from the crease, and hold the two sides flat together with a paperclip. Pairs of names are back to back, so turn the bracelet back and forth to read off the matches. The next day, remove the clip and advance the crease.

The bracelet gives different results with even and uneven numbers because for every jump of the crease one name moves down and another up, passing each other two names at a time. If an uneven number are in the class, the cycle takes in everyone eventually. Advance the crease between the next two names, clip the bracelet, read off the pairs, and repeat daily till all have been matched. One person at the opposite end from the crease is always unpaired. You can partner with that student yourself or make a triad.

Pairing an even-numbered class that way, however, half wouldn't be paired with the other half. Accommodate for that by advancing the names on one side past the names on the other *just one position at a time.* One side of the bracelet in effect holds still while the other moves just to the next name opposite. On alternate days the crease then comes in the middle of a name instead of between two names. When this occurs, instead of creasing through a name, let the names "float" at both ends of the bracelet and match those two together. On the next day the crease is again between two, and on the next day they float, and so on. Eventually everyone is paired with everyone else.

Gradual entry. To change behavior when students are passive, hesitant, or resistant, do so unobtrusively. Engage them in an activity that contains the change you want, arrange for them to succeed at it, and acknowledge their success. They don't notice the change till after it's occurred. They flow with the activity of the moment and find themselves with a new skill.

Put them in the easiest role first from which they can observe others' successful use of a method. Taking a helping role as a questioner in Partner Practice, for instance, they learn the format and subject matter. Counting up and recording their partner's points or time, they learn the scoring method, and giving attention to someone else "doing it right," they increase their confidence that they can do the same. Most are able to imitate a partner readily when the roles are reversed, but some are so withdrawn that they may also need an individualized presentation of the day's lesson: A helper 1) identifies the material to be mastered, 2) checks the student's notebook for questions written separate from answers for easy practice, 3) explains points one by one: "Here are the four points that answer the question . . . ." 4) The student tells the points back immediately. 5) The helper notes a score under that question in the student's notebook, and 6) at the end of the session, sees that scores are added to the student's total on the classroom scoreboard the same as for others (for issues about posting scores, cf. 45). If the student hasn't yet mobilized himself to write the questions and answers, photocopying another's notes is a temporary accommodation.

If transitions between individual and partner work seem unduly time-consuming, cf. "Resolve structure" in 37. Use Maps.

Remedial sessions can be clearly focused: "Learn these five questions and tell them back either to me or to your partner." Provide targets: "We'll cover twenty points today. Please have all the answers copied down, and explain them to your partner without looking at them."

6. Maintain Answers

Be alert to your responses to this section because it may challenge some assumptions. Maintaining answers deliberately instead of allowing them to fade amounts to a paradigm shift. In different eras, educators have emphasized different approaches—here, a conscious, immediate effort to conserve knowledge when it's first presented.

Doing so depends on taking regular time to recall it. This is so fundamental yet so contrary to customary practice that it bears repeating. *If your students aren't saving knowledge and aren't taking regular time to recall it, connect the dots!* The simplest, most direct way for you to insure that they save knowledge is that they recall it. There are many ways to do that—writing, re-writing, re-organizing, speaking to a partner, speaking to a group, testing, performing, structuring, and mentally reviewing. One way or another they have to draw out what's gone in (2). A logical time for this activity is at the start of the same class the day after it's first presented and practiced. They save the prior before adding more, a first step to making it permanent. Whenever they have a day's work well ingested, they use the remaining time to return to prior work to deepen it. Occasionally they can take a full period or more just to practice prior material and incorporate outside learning.

Without an active intent to maintain prior learning, it turns vague. Though the superficiality of much learning hour by hour must be obvious to everyone, schools almost universally implement **the Learn and Lose System.** The pattern enveloping most classrooms leaves behind nebulous learning along the entire scale of ability so that students expect to forget most of what they take in. Even many high on the grading curve are abysmally ignorant. Ten influences designed by adults over which students have little or no control describe their experience:

1. **Courses begin and end by plan**. Students know they won't be called on for their knowledge after the course. Knowing it's over

in a few weeks encourages them to do the minimum and stay on the surface.

2. **No intent to learn a body of knowledge**. Students aren't asked to master a comprehensive explanation but to *qualify*—pass, be eligible for sports, satisfy parents, or obtain further education. Temporary knowledge is enough.

3. Adults wishing to master a subject **keep a complete hard copy**. We buy the book or make detailed notes. In schools, textbooks are returned and notes thrown away. Without them, a student can't update tenuous learning, review is impossible, and fragmented ideas aren't restored to wholeness.

4. **Small pieces** aren't integrated. Exam questions are often atomized into terms, formulas, and parts that aren't conceived as a system with structural harmony.

5. Tests supply the information needed and the student only **recognizes** a correct answer rather than being expected to supply structure and details.

6. **Personal interest is usually irrelevant,** competing with instead of expanding the curriculum. If it's not in the curriculum, it's "no credit." Students conclude that personal interest diverges from education.

7. **Reviews for the test** constrict both the content and the time to focus on it. Near exam time teachers provide a summary of the course from which they draw the test. Just by studying review questions, students can pass respectably, rendering other class hours forgettable.

8. Multiple exams in a brief time **encourage cramming**. A mass of data run through the mind may be unarticulated, disorganized, based on memory alone instead of integrated, and installed under pressure (i.e. by rote), causing it to be lost as rapidly as it was gained. A master teacher mentioned giving the previous semester's final exam to the same students a month later without notice. All suffered a drastic decline in scores and many A grades reverted to F.

9. Courses typically have a **final exam,** which says that this is the last time the school will call on the student to know the subject. Knowledge is released to evaporate.

10. Learning and non-learning are often **accepted equally**. Students with a D grade may receive no followup to bring them to a B or A, so that those at the low end continue to drop out. They need a return loop back to effort that insures results.

Learn and Save. Education's purpose is learning retained, that something should remain in students. The Silver Bullet design offers a clear means: learn, record, and save. Make a hard copy, divide it into questions and answers, practice answering the questions, and maintain them.

To do this while changing nothing else in your teaching methods, just draw all tests from everything you've taught them. The longer students are with you, the more depth and mastery they should have of everything you've worked on together because you test it cumulatively.

You can also make each exam a condensed summary of everything important treated to that point: "You're responsible for a hundred percent score on this test maintained to the end of the term." After the first test, go over all the questions anyone missed and give it again. They continue to retake it until they get a perfect score and then retake it one more time or until you sign them off as having mastered it. Looking forward to this would inspire everyone to study for permanence from the start.

Another way is to revisit course material instead of a specific test. Material from your earliest lessons with them would be fair game for current tests. Half of any test might cover current material and half draw from prior.

In both elementary and high schools, teachers can team up to take advantage of a longer time frame, and hold students responsible for sustaining their learning for two years. One teacher might confirm work begun by several others with either of the designs above. Making all the previous year's material available for inclusion in current tests would largely offset the impact of the Learn and Lose System.

The present design for maintaining learning makes this easier. Because scores are both raised and lowered, students can increase them on their prior courses or decrease them if their test-levels for the material fall off. They could raise any course grade they received in the past two years by re-taking tests and demonstrating further mastery.

Ordinary experience affirms the value of sustained attention to memory. Maybe you've had an experience like mine: I look into an old box of school-related memorabilia and run across old reports, assignments, and collections of information. *Before I pick it up, the material is completely unavailable to my conscious mind.* If I'd wanted it usable throughout my life, even just leafing through it the first week of each January would have been enough. But since I wasn't drawing on it directly and made no effort to recall it, it all disappeared from my mental toolkit. And you—do you retain knowledge without effort, or do you need conscious attention to recalling it?

I have an image of a teacher slapping himself upside the head and saying, "Of course! The reason students don't remember anything is that we don't *ask* them to remember anything. Of course!" Only a deliberate effort to save it turns vague learning into specific.

7. Impromptu Performance

"Performance" here means demonstrating skill or knowledge in front of others, such as by explaining a chunk of learning. Teachers draw on students' needs for attention, acceptance, and approval when they ask questions of them in front of others, but a performance becomes even more significant when a student claims it as a personal achievement; saying in effect, "I'm confident of this and now I'm going to show you." They're invested in demonstrating what they master and not what they know vaguely. Faced with displaying their knowledge publicly, they're stimulated to raise their competence.

For those who'd rather have a sharp stick in the eye than stand up and perform before classmates, we expand their confidence by leading them past their fear in steps. They explain their knowledge to several others one to one until they've mastered it, so that their performances to the class and to their parents are assured successes.

Announce an Impromptu Performance whenever you have a spare three to five minutes. You can 1) ask them to tell back their entire current day's mastered learning, or ask a question 2) from their notebook, 3) from a bag of slips with questions they've learned that day, 4) from a cumulative bag holding all past questions, or 5) from their personal expertise (cf. 40).

Read the question aloud, look at everyone, and pause briefly to hint to them "This could be yours. Are you up to it?" While you count to ten, they draw on their mental stores and call up their knowledge.

Draw a name randomly from a bag of class names to avoid unconscious patterns. Eager students overshadow others and teacher predilections may give unhelpful messages (3). Because it's uncomfortable for us to embarrass or be in conflict with anyone, we typically don't *like* to call on students who we think don't know the answer or who have an off-putting personality trait. Chance selection distributes attention fairly, and drawing from all their names helps prevent anyone from slacking off.

For all to get equal turns at standing and performing, you can set aside their names once they perform until the whole class has done so, and then start over. This leaves an ever larger number coasting, however, knowing they won't be called on. A modification is to fudge. Draw randomly day by day but if you notice one passed over as others repeat, announce his name instead. The student selected stands up, states the question, performs the answer, takes questions from other students if asked, and sits down. Congratulate them and lead the class in applause. Hear from as many as time allows.

An option to consider is to reward everyone with Bonus Time if the questioned student performs competently, which encourages them to support each other's efforts (cf. 28. Use Consequences). Impromptu Performance at the end of a day (especially with a few minutes of Mental Movie, next), sends them out the door with their competence affirmed.

8. Mental Movie

Mental Movie deepens their knowledge and enables them to enjoy thinking about it. Use it whenever you have two to four minutes.

Ask them to sit upright, close their eyes, and calm their breathing. By focusing on the regular inflow and outflow of air, they help their mind enter the alpha brain wave that aids reflective thought. When they find their inner world steady, ask them to "run the movie" of everything they said, did, heard, read, wrote, practiced, performed, and learned from the start of the day as though they were viewing raw footage of a movie about themselves. If they've written a Peg List, they've already placed key ideas in sequence (cf. 29).

Ask them to confirm everything they learned that day and then work backward a day at a time. Attention to four zones may help them: anything visual—images of pictures, diagrams, visible steps, use of board space, and borders around key ideas; sounds of voices; feelings and sensations while they were learning, and specific actions. Knowing that they'll do this later reminds them all day to notice details and to write the script of their movie.

9. Appreciation Time

Many years ago, researchers studying aggressive and cooperative behavior among kindergartners noticed an interesting pattern. They first counted a median of forty-two aggressive acts on the play field daily. Then they introduced a ten minute sharing time when students could tell how others were friendly toward them during play that day, naming another student. There were soon "more buddies than bullies," and the median aggressive acts dropped to nine daily. When they changed the question to ask who was unfriendly toward them, the aggressive acts quickly climbed back to forty per day. Changing once again to naming friendly actions, the median aggressive acts dropped again, this time to six (4).

An exchange only slightly less direct has the same effect on adults. Often in a group setting, I've observed one person refer respectfully to the idea of another—who tends to share more soon after. Others acknowledging our positive action gives us a green light. We feel more secure about our place in the group, and more ready to express the same sort of behavior that brought approval before. With its explicit focus on what's already caused a good feeling, Appreciation Time touches a fundamental need in one with a genuine, credible sentiment in another.

Give your students time each day **to tell how others were friendly, helpful, or kind toward them, or gave them a good feeling (5)**. Address each one individually: "Who gave you a good feeling today?" and "How did they do that?" You can also use an **Appreciation Board**, a small bulletin board where they can write their positive thoughts about each other; thanks, admiration, gratitude, appreciation, help given, and skills they notice others use.

You might think, "My class wouldn't talk about those things."

If they wouldn't, then they especially need to. The harder it is for them to intend others' good feelings and express appreciation, compliment, and thanks, the more they need it. It doesn't occur automatically but only if you arrange it. The class described in Chapter 9 didn't start that way but began fractured and hostile, and in six weeks changed completely.

If you get no response when you invite them to express appreciation, consider their silence a cry of desperation. Think of it. **They're not aware of receiving good feelings from anyone**. Another meaning is just as bad: If they express a good feeling, they fear the treatment they'll get. What an emotional desert, what a depressing situation in which to be forced to spend six hours a day! (Years ago, I visited a fifth grade teacher-friend during her class's recess. As we watched a couple students on the playground, she commented sadly, "About seventy-five percent of the interactions between them are basically cruel.") If some try to sabotage what you attempt, read the deeper message of their fears of self-exposure and their need for emotional safety, and keep at it.

They may find it safer to start distant from the classroom. Refer them to an EXPERIENCE. They've tasted a dessert, taken a warm shower, fallen asleep comfortably, taken a hike on a sunny day.

Then ask, "Why don't we look at THINGS that give you a good feeling?" Brainstorm objects like a bed, food, vehicle, sports equipment, musical instruments, videos, CDs, computer, cell phone, clothes, and so on. Let them fish around for how the use or possession of an object affects them. For those who play a ball game of some kind, a ball in hand changes their state instantly. How would they describe that? Move up the chain toward animate objects: "How about ANIMALS?" How do they describe the feeling they get from petting their cat or playing with their dog? Draw out how their own focus and activity generate the feelings.

"Now how about PEOPLE NOT PRESENT?" Can they think of something someone did for them recently that gave them a good feeling? When they can identify a supportive person, ask them to describe the internal shift that occurs in them around this person. What generates a change? Some will note incidents like interactions during games, but draw out subtle details also like another's smile, the sound of their voice, phrases they use, or attitudes they manifest.

"Now how about anyone PRESENT?" Gradual steps stock their minds for noticing the personal and present. Spend as much time as they can use appreciating those in the room. These comments meet deep-seated needs, remedy hurts, displace feelings of devaluation, and are probably the most powerful force available for changing the atmosphere in your class.

You can personalize the topics in the appendices: "Tell about one of your best experiences with friendship," or "Tell about a time you helped someone who was down." Invite out the specifics of their experience rather than their generalizations.

Some saboteurs may talk about drug/alcohol or violent/destructive experiences, challenging you into opposition that could subvert your relationship with the group. They may hope to test your credibility for talking about good feelings by jarring you into bad ones. You might inquire whether their collective direction will be positive: "Hmm, William. I'm not sure how to respond to that. Let me ask everyone: Do you think you're ready to talk about good feelings and how people give them to each other?" Cues aimed at the distracters are your answer. The topic implies that they're willing and constructive, so you allow them to show you. You might say, "Well, let's try it for a while. If you're not ready for it today, we can go on to the next section in math." (Resume your hardest subject after these sessions if you have a choice.) Other points can help them assimilate appreciation further:

Positive leads to positive, negative to negative. Talk out their experiences of how they carried a tone or attitude from one setting to another, such as school to home or vice versa; or how one person's impact on them affected their relationship with someone else. What developed the tone originally, how was it transferred, and what was the result?

Everyone receives something. Have them count up how much has been provided for them: room, light, heat, paper, pencil, clothing, food, shelter, and so on. Who else had to labor, and where were they in the world for your students to have everything they need? Make lists of what they receive and what they give back to the world, and compare them (6).

Gratitude is the appropriate response for receiving. Let them discuss what they do when they receive from others. Who serves them, and do they respond well or poorly? Gratitude keeps them from viewing themselves as victims. Model it yourself.

Everyone can give something. Ask them to brainstorm what they could give back to the world and to others. Synthesize their discussion into a thoughtful question and answer they record in the Miscellaneous section of their notebook.

How you respond to students personally is likely to arise from an individual style. You may feel naturally involved and readily interact with them, modeling skills easily; or have a natural stance outside the group while tending to its needs. If you're among the latter, a middle ground is to be someone with whom they can practice safely. If they try to involve you in their work on communications or feelings management, play along.

CHAPTER 3

Communicate and Connect

With the basic success structure in place, we can give more refined attention to the relationships students develop. The means below bring rapid results. Students discover that they can connect just by how they give attention and speak positively.

10. Perfect Conversation

On a Monday morning as I stood before my class, fresh in my mind was a gathering I'd attended the night before. A roomful of adults had listened to and built on each other's ideas. "I was in a perfect conversation last night!" I said, and as I described it, I realized that the skills in it could be taught. I wrote them on the board, asked everyone to copy them, and later noted that each skill met a fundamental need:

1   **Look at the speaker > attention**
2   **Leave a brief silence after each one speaks > respect**
3   **Include everyone > inclusion**
4   **Ask questions > being proactive**
5   **Connect with others' ideas > idea development**

My students learned the five points as a Learning Feat, "What are the rules for Perfect Conversation?" Later we made up small groups in which they could practice them. I spurred their motivation by requiring that they complete five minutes using all the skills perfectly before they could break for lunch, which they were able to do easily.

To try it, give everyone a handout or put the rules on the board. Explain and discuss each one and invite them to tell their experience with it, the need it meets, and the effects when it's ignored.

Divide the class into groups of four to six (five may be ideal). Ask each group to sit in a circle so they can see others' faces easily and no one is structurally excluded. Give them a time limit of three to five minutes and say, "See if you can do it." They'll look at each other and scan the guidelines, someone will ask a question, and they're under way. As they're able to use the time, increase it. To monitor several small groups simultaneously, place your chair in the center of the room where you can hear them all.

A reinforcement such as Bonus Time may stimulate them to do the activity perfectly (cf. 28. Use Consequences). If you have them for the period before lunch and can be flexible with your schedule, you might say:

We have twelve minutes before lunch. When your group has done five minutes in which you follow perfectly all five PC rules, give me a signal. If I agree that your group has done it, you can leave early. Pay attention just to your own group. Ignore others if I let them leave early. Each group chooses a timer who keeps track of the group's time and signals to me when you believe you've done your five minutes.

11. Communication Skills Check Sheet

Students seem to work best on communications when they're fresh from contact with others that reminds them that they need it. If time is available soon after lunch, you might alternate then between communications practice and a feelings activity.

Students' skills can change quickly if you 1) explain a skill easy to apply, 2) provide them an experience in which they can practice it, 3) give them explicit recognition for doing so, and 4) continue adding more skills. Both an academic and an experiential approach work, but one may suit you and your students better. Using a variety of means helps develop flexible use of the skills. Make a photocopy of the CSCS (cf. Appendix 9) for their notebooks.

Academic. With students already somewhat disciplined, you can treat the skills like anything else to learn. Divide the Check Sheet into five questions, one for each

What inner activities do you check before communicating?
Notice others' desire to speak.
Feel respect and consideration.
Focus on the one speaking.
Wait until the other finishes

major section, with four to seven points in the answer. Each becomes an independent Learning Feat such as the one boxed here. Daily discuss one CSCS skill thoroughly, but also suggest that they pick one to apply deliberately: "Really put it to work. Plant it in your mind and think how to use it." Younger students can work effectively on a single skill taught to everyone that all practice together. Those older may feel it artificial when everyone roughs in the same unfamiliar behavior, and prefer an individual selection they can employ unobtrusively.

Experiential. You can also create experiences in which they can practice appropriate skills, especially small group discussion. See USE THE

CHECKLIST below for options. Because they involve students more, they may generate more flexibility but also require more time. An alternate is to teach some skills academically and expand practice time as students use it well. Pause for self-checking on the CSCS after any interactive classroom activity and recognize them for skills they use. Model a skill yourself, structure their experience, watch them apply the skill, and let them know what you see.

Check Sheet. I selected the skills on the CSCS by trying various clusters with students of different ages. Some refer to inner activities students aren't accustomed to managing, but learning these along with the outer makes both easier:

1. **What inner activities do you check before communicating?**
    a) *Notice others' desire to speak.* How can you notice that? How do you yourself show that you're ready to speak?
    b) *Feel respect and consideration.* How do these two qualities compare and contrast? What do you do inwardly to feel them?
    c) *Focus on the one speaking.* How do you show that you focus?
    d) *Wait until the other finishes.* How does it feel to wait while another searches for words?

Soon after introducing this set to a class, I arranged a discussion in which I asked them to select a particular skill to use. One caught my attention who typically attempted to distract the class with humor. He was unusually quiet and paid attention. During the debrief, I asked him which skill he'd chosen. "I was feeling respect and consideration," he said solemnly. His focus on a single quality changed both his and everyone else's experience. What struck me from students' comments was their realization that to carry out these steps required effort—to look for cues of others' desire to speak, to open inwardly to a feeling of respect, and to put up with the feeling of waiting. They were startled to notice that they interrupted because they couldn't endure the discomfort of waiting.

2. **How do you listen?**
    a) *Look at the speaker.* How does it feel when others look elsewhere while you talk to them? How can you tell if someone is ignoring you?
    b) *Don't interrupt. Say "Excuse me" if you do.* How do they like being interrupted? What's their experience of having others say "Excuse me"?
    c) *Ask speaker to continue.* How would they do this?
    d) *Leave a brief silence after speaker ends.* With silence after someone speaks, the domination of the discussion by one or a few ceases. People can more easily think about what was said and choose a better response. More are included and feel more respected.

These few guidelines make communication possible. Just looking at the speaker and not interrupting improve primary grade communication vastly. Much of the time students follow these rules automatically, enabling you to affirm their successful practice from the start.

One first grade teacher divided her class into pairs, gave a topic, and asked the speakers to talk for a minute about it. Listeners did points 2a and 2b above, told back two things they remembered, and then traded roles. Within a few minutes, they'd done three rounds with new pairs and topics, and all seemed fascinated, delighted to be universally successful and connecting. The following day a special teacher conducted the class, and afterward asked the regular teacher, "What have you been doing with these children? They're more attentive, they're listening better and cooperating!" The weather was hot and students usually more distracted. Just a few minutes of practice on a single day had caused most to change their behavior. Other first graders benefited from extensive discussion on what it meant not to interrupt.

3. **How do you include everyone?**
   a) *Invite those to talk who haven't.* How do you invite people? What would someone say to you to invite your thoughts? What feelings does it generate?
   b) *Give equal time talking.* How can you do this yourself or help others do it? How does it feel to restrain yourself so someone else can talk?
   c) *Ask questions and accept answers.* What are their experiences, positive or negative, with others asking them questions? Discuss how they can accept answers without agreeing with them.
   d) *Use others' names.* Ask about their feelings of inclusion when they hear their name used.

One of my experimental groups contained fifth graders who had difficulty getting along with others. Just obtaining their willingness to be together and share a few comments constituted success. One day, however, an aggressive girl understood "including others" for the first time. A boy who'd been absent for a couple sessions had returned but was paying no attention. The girl glanced at him, noticed that he was off in his thoughts, said his name, and asked him, "What do *you* think about this?" His eyes changed as though jerked suddenly awake. He answered her question and began to pay attention.

With some students, even such a moment's change is a big gain. Small steps, each done well, eventually draw in all.

4. **How do you give a good feeling?**
   a) *Be interested in what others say.* Hear their experiences of extending and receiving interest.

b) *Ask about their feelings and accept them*. Discuss how they want to have their feelings treated. Do they think others are different?

c) *Thank people*. How do they express gratitude? How do they like to be thanked?

d) *Give compliments*. Explore the range of compliments people can give; how appreciation, admiration, and respect differ, and what makes a compliment welcome or unwelcome.

e) *Tell what helped you*. One of the best ways to give people good feelings is to let them know the positive impact they have on you: "You got my book for me. Thanks." "I could do it the way you explained it."

The intent to give others good feelings is a glue binding a group together. We mobilize it by providing a means to express it and recognition for doing so. Everyone wants to receive good feelings from others, but many don't know how to give them. At a dance once in early high school, I stood near an upperclassman who suddenly began punching me on the arm. Feeling assaulted, I was astonished to learn from his older brother later that he actually had good feelings toward me. Some students are slow to decipher the peer group relationship code. We need to teach them how to exchange good feelings directly.

5. **How can you connect to what others say?**

a) *Remember what others say*. Teach this fundamental intellectual skill by practicing it in pairs and growing to longer remembering (cf. 12. Listen). You want them to exert a conscious decision to remember what's said and done around them, a skill easily mastered.

b) *Use others' words and ideas*. When they state an idea and someone else refers to it respectfully, how do they feel?

c) *Note similarities and differences compared to your ideas*. Discuss how two people's ideas can be partly the same and different, and how they can accept both.

d) *Describe what affects you*. The least intrusive way to lead someone else to change a negative behavior is just to call it to attention. A kindergarten teacher laughed about one of her pupils freezing when she said to him seriously, "Do you realize you're hitting her?" Neutral information can change behavior when blame or criticism could create tension: "The noise makes it hard for me to concentrate." "After I spoke, you changed the subject so I thought you dismissed the point I was making." You simply describe behavior that had an impact on you.

e) *Check out your guesses about others' thoughts and feelings.* Describe their behavior accurately and your guess about its meaning, but don't argue about what you think they feel. They are the authority: "Are you feeling sad? I noticed you frowning." "Did something special happen to you today? You seem really happy."

f) *Summarize others' thoughts and feelings.* Attempt to describe and summarize accurately instead of judging. Practice first with lead-in phrases like, "So you're saying . . . ," "You're feeling . . . about . . . ," "It's important to you that . . . ," "You want . . . ," and "You mean . . .". Let the speaker correct the message: "No, I meant that . . . ."

g) *Talk out problems.* They can describe situations they were in and tell what worked or not to resolve problems (cf. 16. Conflict Resolution).

USE THE CHECK SHEET

1. **Refer to the checklist**. During any small group activity, ask students to place the CSCS on their desks in front of them and refer to it periodically.

2. **Observe**. Ask them to observe others' actions and group incidents, watch for the effect of skills used, and how other skills could have influenced the outcome.

3. **Select skills**. Ask them to select skills they'll use for a day or in an upcoming activity and end with a short debrief afterward: "Which one did you choose? How did it work?" Telling them ahead that they'll comment afterward spurs them to apply what they know.

4. **Rank skills**. Rank the skills in order of their importance.

5. **Add skills**. Ask them to add one skill per day to their repertoire. Invite them to share their experience of using it.

6. **Rate themselves**. Ask them to rate themselves after activities. After small group discussions on Monday afternoons, for instance, they turn to the CSCS in their notebooks and rate their use of each skill or those in a portion you designate. With elementary grades, a 0 to 3 scale is sufficient. 3= excellent use of the skill, 2= moderate use, 1= some use, and 0= not used at all. Upper grades might use 0 to 10. Ask students to leave blank any skill that for some reason didn't apply. A student might rate herself a 10 for "Looked at speaker," because she steadily paid attention to and looked at whoever was talking.

Many students misunderstand how to fill in the boxes, and mark all the columns across the entire page, making them unusable later. To avoid this, draw an example of the sheet on the board.

Point out and explain **what a column is** and the proper one for that day—furthest to the left with no marks in it yet. Explain the rating scale they're to use (e.g. 0 to 3), and talk out examples of the rating levels.

Many students even in high school show that they're parched for approval by giving themselves the maximum score immediately for each skill. They need massive, positive feedback before they can view themselves objectively. Just continue providing new occasions for ratings, and allude to a realistic perspective: "It's fun to rate your own actions, isn't it? Sometimes you can learn a lot."

7. **Rate others**. When you have a series of small group discussions with ongoing groups, shift the manner of their rating from day to day. First they put their name at the top of the sheet and rate themselves. The next day, they hand their sheet (or notebook if they've inserted it there) to their left, **rate the person whose name is on the sheet given to them,** and then hand it back. Third day, they hand it to their right, again rate the person whose name is at the top, and on the fourth day, hand it across the group. Comparing their self-rating with how others rate them increases their objectivity.

8. **Use a skill overnight**. They apply a skill at home overnight, and the next day discuss the results of their effort.

9. **Write feedback**. On a poster, they write others' names and the skills they observed them use.

10. **Practice reciprocity**. To lead into a discussion of accurate understanding, suggest a game they know like football, softball, or basketball that includes throwing and catching. Explain it as an analogy for communication, and invite their experiences of "when the ball was dropped" and why:
    Throwing and catching must be equal. If someone throws, someone else needs to catch or the ball is lost. You catch and throw an equal number of times and you throw to where the catcher is, not out of bounds where they can't get it. So adjust your words to what the other is ready to receive. And when you're the receiver, try to catch the meaning the other wants to send.

11. **Skill tally**. Pick out eight to ten communication skills important enough that you want students to receive daily feedback on them. To involve them in the selection, invite them to rate each skill on the CSCS on a 0-10 scale for its importance (or reach group consensus) and use those they choose. Make a Content Scoreboard (cf. 47) with the same number of columns and write a skill at the head of

each column with student names down the side. When you see a student using a skill, make a tally mark in the square beside the student's name and under the skill without interrupting the lesson. At the end of the period, call attention to the skills tallied. Allow students to make tallies for others, or select a couple at random who do tallies for that period (cf. also 42).

12. **Debrief**. When you assign a communications task to students, always include a debrief, even just for a minute. They describe what happened, rate their skill, or hear another's perception of their effort. If you ask them to try something they know you won't check on later, many will nod agreeably and forget it. The debrief is essential to the learning loop.

STUDENTS CHOOSE

For students edgy about cooperating, engage them in creating their own checklist. You can invite them to brainstorm how they want others to act toward them, and vote for their top ten suggestions. If they complain, they make a point about how they want things to be, so you extract that element: "So that's what you don't want. What does it imply that you do want?" Turn around semantically negative statements into their implied positive. "I hate it when people interrupt me" becomes "I like people to let me finish my thought." "Letting people finish" then goes on their list to practice (7). By identifying skills they'd like to post, they've already focused on each one, assessed its importance, and subconsciously bought into the idea of practicing it.

Let them observe their interactions with each other and their families for several days and describe skills they might want to include. Discuss their findings, combine the similar, make a checklist, duplicate it or mount it on a poster, and use it with the suggestions in the preceding section.

12. Listen

Communicating is easy to teach with a modicum of cooperativeness, a clear map, the opportunity to practice, and recognition afterward. We start with a simple design and build more refined perceptions into it. With just a few minutes a day at the next exercises, students learn to connect with others just by speaking and listening. If you think negative attitudes could interfere with the exercises, you might employ Appreciation Time for awhile first (cf. 9).

The beginning is basic recall. They hold in mind a little of what they hear. Tell them "We're going to practice listening and just remembering what others say. If you can do that, you can learn from everyone else's good ideas." Instruct them not to comment. One teacher told first grade listeners, "Zipper your mouth so you won't interrupt," and they did so with dramatic gestures.

Select topics most can speak to; more tangible ones for the younger: food, movies, games, pets, yards, their room, common experiences, and favorite categories of things. Appendices 2-5 have suggestions for different ages.

For many, having any answer is more important than an original answer. A trainer who'd taken many small groups through a leadership course gave me a clue about this. At first, he said, he wanted his adult male participants to supply their own answers to his questions. In time he found it more effective to have a prepared phrase for them to express in their own words. Training them was less about originality than about focus, just getting them to pay attention to a way of thinking.

If some appear unable to speak spontaneously about a topic, you can brainstorm a class answer from which they can draw their own: "Here's what we've gathered from the class. When you talk in pairs, mention the part that appeals to you personally." As they feel safe and successful, individualized answers emerge.

Use your assigned daily partners for this exercise if you have them (cf. 5), but for the extremely shy or self-conscious, even talking in pairs may be too demanding. Ask them individually to sit beside a couple who "know how to do it" and watch "until you get the idea." Expect them to resolve their hesitance quickly. After others model for them once or twice, shift them to a pair. Offer a simple rule to determine who talks first, such as the one whose first name is first in the alphabet.

To start off, little time is needed for each turn; for first graders a minute or two and older students more. Increase the time as they accept each other, cooperate with new partners, and give each other good attention.

After speakers' time ends, listeners recall what they heard. The little they draw from each others' words is still significant as the first sign of their ability to absorb others' thoughts.

The content you ask for varies. Primary students tell back *one thing they can remember* from what the speaker shared. Upper elementary, talking for a longer time, might select two or three points. Older students might try to summarize everything. With short time spans, everyone succeeds and increases their confidence in their listening ability.

When recall is done, recognition confirms the success *of the listener*. Ask students to raise their hands if their listening partner was able to recall what you asked them to.

The reason for doing this is that student speakers typically don't think of the other person as the main actor. They focus on themselves. By placing attention on their partner's accomplishment, you stretch their world and make them a source of recognition for each other. If two behaviors make an activity work, in other words, and the loss of either causes it to fail, then sensibly we encourage the weaker; between speaking and listening, typically the latter. Most of its effort is internal and invisible in selecting, impressing within, and then recalling another's ideas. Speaking, on the other hand, they do automatically, but to improve at thinking about what to say, most children also need superior listening that welcomes their thoughts. So we don't want just speaking, but rather *speaking to good listeners.* If listening is good, the speaker's success is assured.

Many enjoy keeping score of the one thing they recalled in listening. Make a wall chart listing their names and a space beside each for a series of tallies, one for each point they remembered from their speaker.

If you prefer not to have individual scores, use an all-class score. Tape a six inch wide strip of paper from floor to ceiling with two lines on it an inch apart up the center of it, forming an empty column. For every point anyone recalls from their partner's sharing, blacken the column from the floor upward for an eighth of an inch. Recall of one point by twenty students generates a two and a half inch rise in the bar.

A lifetime lesson is embedded in their activity. Ask them, "Why do we remember what others say? What happens when we don't?" Invite their stories about ignoring others' words or forgetting what they agreed to.

To teach them the model, do three rounds in rapid succession, assigning different partners each time. This sets up a mental map, zaps resistance, breaks down cliques, expands the friendship network, and increases their confidence that they can do what you expect of them.

13. Total Attention

The listening proposed above began with the easily monitored behavior of recalling what others say. Next is developing caring presence to each other. Many are uncertain how to express supportive feelings and don't realize the power of attentive presence.

Prepare for total attention pairs by having students learn and tell back the first set of skills on the Communication Skills Check Sheet, "What inner activity do you check before communicating?" Discuss how they notice others' desire to speak, give respect and consideration, and wait. The third section of the CSCS, "How do you give a good feeling?" is also helpful.

Explain the goal of giving good attention to another. It can be difficult because it asks us to relinquish associations that spring up in our own mind. Someone says "I went to the beach" and they're flooded with thoughts of their own beach experiences, and want to tell about them. They need to prevent their mind from flitting through their own memories and ceasing to listen. Trying instead to develop in mind only what the other says about their beach amounts to a continuous sacrifice. Their turn will come, but in the meantime they turn attention from their own inner world and open instead to the picture the other paints in them.

To familiarize them with it, model what you want. Sit facing a single student volunteer, allow he or she to begin, and immerse entirely in what they say. Let your facial expression, posture, nods, and body position reveal listening. Adopt an inward attitude of acceptance, of not judging. Show respect for the student, and become fascinated at their world. Then ask everyone to list what they saw you do, and inquire of the speaker how it felt to receive this kind of attention. You might write down their observations as a checklist they can refer to when they give total attention to each other. Explain how they can construct inwardly what a speaker says, and then let them try it.

Inquire if they'd like to choose a topic ahead of time (cf. 14). It doesn't limit them but is a jump-off for exploring what they wish.

Suggest that when speakers finish, listeners respond with compliments, appreciation, or admiration, and how they were personally helped by anything they heard.

The speaker, in return, reinforces the listener's attentiveness by telling what helped the speaker most and ignoring anything unhelpful. Discuss with everyone how others' listening makes it easier to stay on track.

Total attention with silence. The next stage is attention that's not just *good* but *total,* non-judgmental, and non-intrusive. It generates safety and well-being in which peaceful reflection can emerge. It permits the speaker to be silent and for the inner consciousness to *be* before it must *do*; to rest in a steady flow of support before it must expend energy toward developing ideas. Some students may feel anxious with silence at first because our culture trains them into constant activity. Provide alternate imagery:

As you take your turn and talk to your partner, think of laying on the side of a grassy hill on a warm day looking at the different shapes of the clouds. You and the person with you stop for a rest after an activity. There's nothing you have to do. You can bring out a thought, talk about it, think a while, bring out another thought, look at the clouds, say something else. The other listens without interrupting, just letting you explore whatever comes to your mind. After you talk a while, the other does the same. We're in a classroom instead of on a grassy hill, but we can think and talk with no pressure at all just as if we were outside in the sun. We'd like to take two hours to do this, but we'll start with small amounts of time first and build from there as you're able to use the time. Please pair up and decide who is the first *receiver* of attention and the first *giver* of attention. (Wait till that's done). **Now I ask the giver of attention to pay attention to the other in a general, overall way without expecting nor judging anything. Your job is just to absorb and appreciate this person. Receivers of attention, for this first round, I'll ask you not to share anything out loud in words. You only *think* while the other pays attention to you. Just watch your thoughts come and go and allow the other person to give attention to you. There's nothing you need to do to earn it, nothing you need to say. Just be who you are and allow the other to notice you. Relax and enjoy it. Please do this for one minute. Any questions? Ready? The minute starts NOW.**

After a minute, debrief the experience with them. It generates subtly different ways of looking at their inner world. Start with those receiving the attention and hear their answers to questions like the following:

In a minute, we'll reverse roles, so you'll get to play the other part. But for this round let's talk first with those receiving the attention. Receivers, how did you react inside? Was it hard or easy to relax? Was it hard or easy to accept the other's attention? Was it hard to restrain yourself from talking? Can you name the feeling it gave you? Can you identify any way your partner helped you even though he or she wasn't talking? Now to the givers. Givers of attention, what was hard and what was easy? Was it hard not to talk? Was it hard not to expect anything or make judgments? What did you notice about the receiver? Share with your partner now any positive thoughts that went through your mind, or any way you found a benefit from the exercise.

Have them reverse roles in the same pairs without talking and again debrief their experience in the new role.

Total attention with talking. In previous exercises listeners learned to recall what the other said, and then to bring their inner world quietly present to the speaker's world. They learned to withhold talking about their own ideas and restrained the urge to say, "I did that too!" Now dismissing all their own thoughts, listeners aim just to absorb fully the picture that the speaker develops, and allow their imagination to be taken by the hand wherever the speaker wishes to lead. Give them a time limit and ask them to begin.

This sort of caring, undistracted attention has a powerful effect. As people probe the edges of their thoughts, others' acceptant attention sustains them in a way that it doesn't when they feel hurried or judged. Speakers learn to assemble their own thoughts without depending on others, and become better able to weigh their own ideas and experiences, shift perspective, and notice the impact of feelings. *The essential quality of the experience that enables them to do this is realizing they won't be criticized nor analyzed but accepted as they are.*

Once everyone understands how to offer this kind of attention, allow speakers five minutes to talk and increase the time gradually. To extend their understanding, discuss conditions that enhance it:

Respect and consideration

Privacy, not telling others what their partner said

Giving good feelings

Not applying labels

Developing their own ideas, images, and experiences

Non-intrusion versus intrusion of others' ideas into theirs

When and how they have thoughtful silences with friends

Looking always for the positive versus looking for the negative

Seeing what they can learn from others

Fascination at how others build and decorate their inner world

Discrimination about what they want to talk about to a partner

With younger classes you may presume that they keep confidences and not even raise the possibility of breaches of trust. From mid-elementary onward they may have had their confidences misused and welcome discussion about how it feels to have others talk about their words and actions, and how they treat others' personal information. If you think caution is advisable, say, "In our discussions, there's no reason to talk about anything that puts someone down or could embarrass anyone else or yourself."

14. Select and Explore Topics

Selecting topics for group or class discussion enables students to think about what concerns them. The more committed they are to the topic, the more they cooperate in skill-building with it. Knowing the topic enables them to reflect on what they want to say, and a collective focus helps them clarify and remember their conclusions more easily.

Weighed against these benefits is the value of free association. Their minds may not wish to go A-B-C, but rather A-G-Z, surfacing what matters most but by an unforeseeable route. Either way, with a teacher's competent moderating, open discussions can have a powerful effect. Although you may start with a selected topic, listen for divergent comments and allow participants to decide together if they want to follow them out. Select topics in several ways:

Topic areas. Fill the writing board with topics they'd like to talk about (or refer them to the lists in the Appendix). Less self-conscious classes can go to the board and make tally marks beside the ten they want. Doing this in writing instead gives everyone cover from revealing their worries publicly and prevents any students from dominating. All write down their top ten for you to tally.

Many topics are important for addressing fears, unfamiliar situations, and issues they're growing into handling. A topic's urgency to them may be far beyond their ability to think it through, such as middle school students wanting to discuss boy-girl relationships. It may help to have more than one topic available, and for them to know they can return to significant ones as they discover more they can say. Make up a list all agree on, post it, and schedule topics accordingly.

One direction is to ask them questions like those listed in 26. Life Knowledge without providing an answer. They figure out theirs, you add in yours and/or the book's, and together devise a comprehensive version.

The Appendix contains several lists with a wide range of age relevance and challenge. Students can nominate from these lists and either reach consensus by discussion, or vote for those that they want.

When they're fluid at developing thoughts together, try out advanced topics that have multiple meanings and metaphorical associations (Appendix 5). Arrange groups and then ask a student to pick one for the class by touching the list with a pencil with his eyes closed. He announces it and the groups start. If you want to work regularly with these, duplicate the Appendix, cut it into as many equal pieces as you have students, and let them write each topic on a separate slip. Collect the slips into a sack, and when you announce groups again, draw one randomly.

Spontaneity and prior reflection emphasize different skills. Sometimes preparing for discussion can encourage deeper thought. A day ahead, ask them to write out their thoughts about the topic and bring them to their group. Everyone shares what they've written so that each one's ideas receive acceptance before discussing any of them, moderating the influence of dominant students. If reflection is more important, consider having them prepare but otherwise use their skills as ideas come to their minds. The rough form of a haphazard grade school discussion morphs through the years into a thoroughly-prepared post-graduate seminar.

The seven questions below can help them explore a topic. You can let them place the list in front of them to refer to during small group discussions, but since it's likely to be useful to them throughout their lives, have them also master it as a Learning Feat.

1. *What's your first thought on hearing the topic?* Draw on everyone's free association, inviting their first mental picture or memory. This alerts everyone to similarities and differences and opens many tangents for examination. To accustom them to *having* a first thought, suggest that they notice how they start thinking about it, notice what comes up first. Use the list of advanced topics to practice: Announce one, wait a few seconds, and do a Consult (cf. 21) on the very first thought, word, or picture that arises in each

one's mind. Do this rapidly several times in a row until everyone catches onto having a first thought.

2. *What experiences have you had about the topic?* If their story is heard, students feel accepted.

3. *What feelings does the topic bring up?* Hearing each others' feelings in response to the topic expands social/emotional learning. They need rich and detailed knowledge about how issues affect people.

4. *What different meanings does the topic have?* Explore literal and figurative meanings, and the topic as metaphor. "Mountain" can refer to a topographical feature, a challenge in one's life, or what one makes out of a molehill. Unfolding the meaning associated with a topic is the work of discussion.

5. *What's most important to you about the topic?* Explore how it could impact their lives or connect them with others.

6. *Do you have a question related to the topic?* Topics are often important because of how their unknowns may affect us and so are often incomplete or unclear. Let students think what they want to discover.

7. *What action can you foresee* someday that relates to the topic? Though it may be far in the future, they may make their first choices about it in your classroom.

15. Discussion Groups

Managing discussions intensively as we suggest below responds to the pressure to accomplish more in less time, and to students' need for guidance as they rough in unfamiliar behaviors.

1. **Forming groups.** Form groups of three to six students. The more participants in each, the greater is the competition for talking time, so the more effective they must be with communication skills. Four or five in a group is a good starting number for most classes, while younger children need larger numbers in an adult-led group. When you feel they're ready to work semi-independently, ask them to join with others nearby. Modify the groups as needed to account for those who either don't get along or could help each other.

Let their level of confidence guide you in how many days to leave the groups intact. Students uncertain, shy, and monosyllabic need longer to get comfortable in a group, several days or more. If they're confident and communicate easily, the stimulation of a shifting membership even daily may suit them better. In general, build trust and safety before versatility, and let them gain ease in talking in one group before changing group configuration.

2. **Choose a topic**. Explain the reasons for selecting a topic, and engage them in generating a list from which they draw one for the day. For variety, you might also announce "No topic today" so they can practice developing ideas spontaneously. The seven questions above for exploring topics can help them enter the discussion while their confidence grows. As they relax, they need such suggestions less.

3. **Plan skill use.** We want them respectfully developing ideas others offer. Ask them to choose skills they'll use to achieve this (e.g. by consulting the CSCS), and how they'll check their use afterward. Explain any skill you especially want them to practice.

4. **Set a time limit and run it**. In the beginning, keep the time short. When they can include everyone during an eight-minute discussion with good skills, consider extending it. Eventually they'll use a full period productively, but at the start intervene right away if the activity deteriorates.

    The four rules above generate a discussion, but debriefing steps afterward enhance its quality. Use no more than two of the following four steps 5-8 on any day; one of either five or six, and/or one of either seven or eight. The first pair reinforce the development of the process, and the second the assimilation of the content. Knowing that they're expected later to rate skills, give feedback, remember, or summarize the discussion gives them a reason to pay better attention.

5. **Check their skills**. Use the CSCS for feedback after the discussion as explained above (cf. 11). They can alternate rating themselves or someone else on their use of the skills.

6. **Verbal feedback**. Once they know what the skills are, growth lies in the choice to use them—which their comments to each other powerfully influence. For the one receiving it, a smile, a reference to their contribution to the group, or a phrase describing a skill they used adds to their self-understanding and confidence. They may also note positive contributions: "You asked a question that helped draw out his idea," "You helped her tell about her feeling," "You gave a really clear example." Invite them to note each person's contribution, and how someone used a skill toward them. Even a bare minute of this at the end of a discussion makes a difference.

7. **Recall of content**. Knowing they'll recall the content later makes them more aware of it during the discussion. Divide them into pairs, and ask them to tell back to a partner "who said what," or "everything said in the group," or "a summary of the discussion," or "the most important points." One partner can attempt the whole thing (switching on alternate days), or they can each take half the

time, in two minutes easily summarizing everything they'd want to retain from the discussion. There's no better way to install an insight than to remember others' specific comments about it. Connecting details to the person who spoke them gives them more relevance that does a spare-boned generalization.

8. **Write questions and answers**. Writing sustains insights but takes more time. Use it when groups discuss academic content or when their conclusions could be valuable to them later. You might ask them 1) to identify the question(s) their discussion answered, 2) write the question on the Questions page of the appropriate notebook section and 3) the answer in the Answers section. They could 4) work together to summarize an ideal answer, 5) include some of each student's sharing in it, and 6) let everyone copy the result.

9. **Managing discussions**. If a student hinders his group, place him back from it but close enough to hear. Tell him, "Just absorb what they're doing till you get the hang of it." He makes this adjustment best when he's placed where he has nothing else to do but observe others' model of cooperation while still feeling connected to the group. A location half in and half out appears to serve best. When he says he understands, return him to the inner circle.

Observe what's happening. The noise level when you see everyone participating sounds like a high hum, revealing that they're enjoying the experience. It's a light sound without brassy exclamations, raucous laughter, nor putdowns that might cause some to withdraw.

Note body position. When people are interested, they usually lean forward to hear better. Groups become more compact. As you see body position spreading out or turning aside, the group connection is weakening. Do they look at the speaker?

Note facial expression, preferably animated, mobile, and changing congruently with the flow of meaning. As it dulls to a masklike appearance or eyelids droop, they're losing energy.

Listen in. Are they still on the subject, reflecting more deeply, using words accurately, or reflecting superficially? If they might benefit from continuing, ask them quietly, "Are you done or do you want more time?" Ideally, you'd like them so immersed in their discussion that they don't hear you.

16. Conflict Resolution

At the African-American Academy that welcomed my pilot program (cf. Chapter 9), Mr. Dawson, the fourth grade teacher, caught me excitedly one day as I walked in during a break. He indicated a boy in the far corner of the room.

"He's been one of the worst in starting fights on the playground," he said. "Hardly a day would go by without a fight." I glanced at the boy. In class he'd participated like the others in communication skills practice, feelings discussions, and Learning Feats.

"Today the boys were playing a game outside during lunchtime," the teacher continued. "They got into an argument and were shouting at each other. I went over closer because that kind of thing would always break down into fighting before. This time I heard him reflect back what the other was saying, 'So you're saying that . . .' and the other student picked it up and they started talking about it. And in a few minutes they solved it and were back playing the game!" He grinned broadly. It had been a tough year for them to that point, and we were making a difference.

If your class needs extra practice in conflict resolution, select skills from the CSCS or from the two lists below. Demonstrate them, add others you like, discuss them thoroughly, and practice them as a Learning Feat. The Content Scoreboard (cf. 47) can help students track their mastery of the skills.

Give seven skills for solving conflicts.

1 **Feel respect and consideration.**
2 **Ask questions.**
3 **Ask about their feelings.**
4 **Describe what affects you.**
5 **Check out your guesses about others' thoughts and feelings.**
6 **Summarize others' thoughts and feelings.**
7 **Talk out problems.**

Give five steps for talking out problems (8).

1 **What is the problem? (Develop a statement that includes how everyone sees it.)**
2 **What have we tried? (Uncover prior statements of the problem and efforts toward it.)**
3 **How did it work? (Identify results and reflect on them).**
4 **What else can we try? (Involve everyone in brainstorming a list.)**
5 **What will we do next? (Listen carefully to talk out what works for all.)**

17. Use Ratings

We carry a process forward as we sustain in mind a reason for doing so. When we notice a different reason, it leads us to a different activity. This implies that to get students to change, we need to make a reason conscious to them and then enable them to envision the outcome of focusing on it.

Rating a quality of the classroom is one way to hold a reason in mind. It's relevant to them because it's a quality of their experience already, and how they think about it today may affect their experience tomorrow.

Rate You. You can begin their training in communication skills by asking them to rate your listening ability. Just say,

I want to improve my listening. At the end of the day, I'll give you a blank slip of paper. Write on it a number from zero to ten and turn it in. Ten would mean I listened almost perfectly to you, I understood your feelings, your needs, and your ideas very well. Five means I was so-so in listening, and zero means I didn't listen at all.

Pay attention then to how you listen. Repeat back their ideas to clarify what they mean. Look at them when they speak, move closer, adjust your voice tone and pace to theirs, lower your eye level to match theirs, and follow their train of thought. Then at the end of the day, you can invite them to tell what they observed about your listening. Let their written ratings be anonymous, since they may also reveal how students feel about you or the class in general. Post the average in a box you draw on the writing board or list it by dates. When you have several, make a line chart and plot your scores proceeding upward across it (assuming you're improving in their eyes). They'll notice that this appears interesting and achievable, a map they can follow.

Rate class overall. Identify classroom qualities they can influence and ask them to rate the measures selected 0-10. If you've already demonstrated listening and had them practice it, you might start with *How well did others listen to me?* Cut scratch paper into small squares and distribute them before the close of class. They do the rating and drop the slips in a jar as they leave. Five others are:

How well did I support others? On alternate days you can switch to *How well did others support me?* Charting their respective answers (e.g. with different colored lines on the same chart) can stimulate discussion and remind them of changes they want to make. If they rate themselves as supporting others at 8 and the next day receive support at 4, the difference deserves examination. Maybe the class needs more Appreciation Time and a discussion of how people often perceive the same thing differently. The rating activity awakens awareness of their attitudes of accepting, helping, and being kind to each other. Enlist a student volunteer to add, average, and post the scores. You can also place a dot above and below the average to mark the highest and lowest scores reported.

How much effort did I expend? (How hard did I try?) Discuss concentration, complacency, mood variances, staying on task, and restoring their enthusiasm.

How well did we take charge of our learning? Ask students to measure themselves on this criterion when they undertake classroom organization teams (cf. 18). The more methods in learning, memory, and cooperation they can use independently, the higher this score can be.

How interesting did we make learning today? This question presumes that students have independent initiative and that you allow them to help design their learning.

Without telling them its significance to you, you can also ask them to measure their progress on some of the criteria showing the effects of the Silver Bullet design (cf. Baseline Data in Chapter 10). Normally you'd want such progress to remain unconscious, but deliberate self-rating is basic to the design. They're encouraged to know that the number of fights or the amounts of litter have dropped.

The **Progress Ladder** (Appendix 8) integrates several continua that mark students' growing maturity, self-direction, and emotional balance. They enjoy estimating their gradual shift from one category to another. Make a copy for them to insert in their notebooks, and weekly ask them to score themselves. I've found that they usually do so quite accurately, but if you notice a rating unrealistically high or low, discuss with the student individually, "What features of this combined rating do you feel you're strong and weak in?"

18. Organization Groups

Responsibility emerges best in small groups directing their own efforts. They show they're ready for it through their progress in acceptance, communications, and giving good feelings to each other. Academic and developmental purposes unite as learning becomes the means by which they meet their needs for inclusion and mutual influence. We teach them skills for aiding and affirming each other, and arrange for their expression in a learning situation. Granting them management of more of their learning then becomes possible.

Designing the groups. For organization groups to aid students' learning and development, their composition is more significant than with discussion groups you reconfigure frequently (cf. Chapter 9 for an example). It matters that members help each other, don't rub others the wrong way, and support the one who most needs it. Forming groups by random drawing can load one with problems while others burst with talent, so if you begin this way, notice if strategic shifts can balance the groups before you announce them.

Asking students' help, on the other hand, can guide you in designing the best experience for students you worry about. First, all write their name at the top of a piece of paper, and draw a line down the middle of it. On one side, titled *Be With*, they list those with whom they'd like to be in a group. They title the other *Learn From,* and list those they think they could best learn from.

If they ask "How many can we name?", leave it up to them. The more they name, the more comfortable they are in class and the more likely they're the kind of bridging person you want to find. Assure them that you're the only one who'll see their list, and ask them not to talk to others about their nominations.

When you're alone, make up a spreadsheet with namers down the left side and the same list across the top as namees to identify who selected whom. With one sheet at a time, note the student who compiled it whose name is at the top. Go to his/her name on the namer list on the left side of your spreadsheet. To the right of his/her name place a tally mark under each of those he/she lists, and total up the columns under each student name.

Identify first the students named least, those with the fewest total tallies under their names, whom others chose the least to be with or learn from. These are the class rejects, the nervous ones who expect hurts from others. Note whom they tallied, and find among these the ones named most. These are the bridging people, the ones they like who are also popular with others. Give them their top choices of those students, especially if they were chosen in return. You want to join the most needing students with those with whom they immediately experience harmony. Assign the remainder to balance ability and cooperation and to respect their choices.

Assign captains. Among those you regard as the best leaders, note which are named most by the students, and combine the group's judgment with your own. Call them whatever fits their frame of reference: captain, big beetle, alpha dog. Expand the meaning of their role by asking them to find in their social studies all the ways that organizations designate leaders and what they do. Suggest a mission for them such as "to assure learning and harmony in my group." Teach them actions they can apply right away and consult with them regularly on how they carry them out:

helping their group organize materials and notebooks
assigning daily practice partners within their group
dividing up projects or assignments, giving each a part to do
monitoring the accuracy of their members' scores in time and points
adding up and posting members' scores on class scoreboards
suggesting ways of rating their group's progress
reporting results to you
solving problems that arise between group members
thinking of ways to increase interest in learning
receiving supplies from a class Supplies Captain and accounting for them
signing out their group to the library or for other special projects and being accountable for their behavior
cooperating with other group captains on projects or study

Add responsibilities slowly until their group works as an independent unit. Form the captains into a team to run the classroom all the ways they can, and suggest that they apply to their group the model you apply to them: ask people to do what they're able to do and back them up.

Be ready to intervene early. The initial need is for each student to find a place, an experience of acceptance. Until this happens, learning is impaired for the one not accepted. Divert ineffective strategies: "Joe, I noticed that you (did such and such), and then . . . happened. Would you like to try something that might work better? What can you think of doing differently? Here's a suggestion."

If clashes occur in the first groups, do what's easiest for the most vulnerable. The deeper their personal needs, the more important it is to build support around them. If you must move someone, choose someone else. They've already experienced not fitting in and this is already one more hurt. Move others instead who are flexible—the constructive closer and the destructive further away—and try to leave target students where they find reassurance.

How long to maintain group composition depends on their needs and your goals. Entering a different group, they practice establishing themselves with new people, yet you also want their productivity from clicking as a team. A middle ground is probably between two and four weeks. After three weeks, you might be guided by having them write what they learned from being in their group. Sometimes you can shift leaders in the same group; appoint them yourself while hearing the captain's recommendation for a successor, or let the first leader select and train a lieutenant who takes over next. How they change leaders can occasion a discussion of such roles in family and society.

Three ways to use the groups for learning are for discussions, dividing subjects (cf. 41), and paired work. Groups of four provide each person with three others to pair with, balancing variety with continuity and support.

CHAPTER 4

Teach Self-Management

Students' attitudes affect how they learn and relate to others. Teachers can influence them through direct contact, teaching self-management skills, and arranging for students to influence each other's feelings and behavior.

19. Appreciation List

Any of us can verify the lasting power of appreciation by recalling when we received it ourselves. An example is a story circulated on the Internet without attribution that I pass on as received:

One day, a teacher asked her students to list the names of the other students in the classroom on a sheet of paper, leaving a space between each name. Then, she told them to think of the nicest thing about each of their classmates and write it down. It took the remainder of the class period to finish this assignment, and as the students left the room, each one handed in his paper. That Saturday, the teacher wrote down the name of each student on a separate sheet of paper and listed what everyone else had said about that individual. On Monday, she gave each student his or her list. Before long, the entire class was smiling. "Really?" she heard whispered. "I never knew that I meant anything to anyone!" and "I didn't know others liked me so much," were most of the comments. No one ever mentioned those papers in class again. She never knew if they discussed them after class or with their parents, but it didn't matter. The exercise had accomplished its purpose. The students were happy with themselves and one another. That group of students moved on.

Several years later, one of the students was killed in Vietnam, and this teacher attended his funeral. She had never seen a serviceman in a military coffin before. He looked so handsome, so mature. The church was packed with his friends. One by one, those who loved him took a last walk by his coffin. The teacher was the last one to bless the coffin. As she stood there, one of the soldiers who acted as pallbearer came up to her.

"Were you Mark's high school math teacher?" he asked.

She nodded, "Yes."

Then he said, "Mark talked about you a lot." After the funeral, most of Mark's former classmates went together to a luncheon. Mark's mother and father were there, obviously waiting to speak with this teacher. "We want to show you something," his father said, taking a wallet out of his pocket.

They found this on Mark when he was killed. We thought you might recognize it." Opening the billfold, he carefully removed two worn pieces of notebook paper that had obviously been taped, folded, and refolded many times. The teacher knew without looking that the papers were the ones on which she had listed all the good things each of Mark's classmates had said about him.

"Thank you so much for doing that," Mark's mother said. "As you can see, Mark treasured it." All of Mark's former classmates started to gather around. Charlie smiled rather sheepishly and said, "I still have my list. It's in the top drawer of my desk at home." Chuck's wife said, "Chuck asked me to put his in our wedding album." "I have mine too," Marilyn said. "It's in my diary." Then Vicki, another classmate, reached into her pocketbook, took out her wallet and showed her worn and frazzled list to the group. "I carry this with me at all times," Vicki said and without batting an eyelash, she continued, "I think we all saved our lists." That's when the teacher finally sat down and cried. She cried for Mark and for all his friends who would never see him again . . . we forget that life will end one day. And we don't know when that one day will be . . .

Your thoughtful, personal feedback can impact a student: "I've been thinking about what you did in class the other day, and I wanted to mention that it stood out in a couple ways . . . ." This implies that 1) you were worth thinking about, 2) I looked deeper into you, and 3) I found positive meaning. Your message is more believable when it comes from your genuine reflection. Acknowledgment of their outer accomplishment has passed and a more personal thought arrives. People treasure discernment that lets them know they're truly seen and that what's seen is valued.

20. Finding Good

Sometimes students' unacceptable behavior shakes our balance. We disapprove and are tempted toward negative comments. We also know we can alienate students and make misbehavior more likely, yet if we ignore it and suppress our antipathy, the student may think we cave in.

We want them instead to know that we're on their side even if we must discipline them. We accomplish this by offering an accurate *but positive* perception of the student's *negative* behavior. We look deeper into the negative to find a positive in it. We don't excuse it or ignore the need for a consequence but rather say, "I see good in you even though your use of it is against our rules." **There's a quality in the student that's either neutral at worst or fundamentally good that we can respect. Once we acknowledge that, we deal better with its current improper use**.

The paragraph in each situation below initiates perhaps a ten-minute problem-solving session with the student. Your aim is to generate understanding while sustaining the bridge between you. Younger ones might need only a sentence or two of it:

A student **talks to** other students during your presentation, diverting from the subject matter and distracting others. You're frustrated and annoyed. In the past you may have made a comment to the student that he or she resents.

Talking to others is an innate, positive human activity. Through it we connect to others and meet our needs. After class you might face the student, get his attention up close, and say, "Jerome, I notice that you like to talk to people. This is a good thing you'll do for the rest of your life. It's important to be able to connect with people around us. People express their friendship and help each other when they talk. The problem is that doing it during class while I'm trying to explain something makes it harder for you and everyone to listen and follow. Do you understand the problem? So I'd like to ask you to notice the feeling of wanting to talk. When that feeling comes up, tell yourself that you can do it later. Would you try that? Try to sense the desire coming up inside you before you say something. Instead of talking then, save what you want to say for later. Tomorrow I'll ask you if you experienced that desire and how you handled it."

A student's **sarcastic comment** about another student causes others to laugh. Because you hate to see anyone hurt, this upsets you and your first instinct is to level the one who made the comment.

Privately and quietly look for a positive within the negative, such as "Aaron, you have an ability I respect. I think it will help you throughout your life. It's your feel for words. Sometimes you can find a word that expresses perfectly what you want to say, and this will be a big asset to you. All your life it may help you make others laugh. What's not acceptable here, however, is that your humor can make another feel bad. That makes it not worth it. Getting a laugh by making someone feel bad tends to come back on us eventually and drives good people away from us. They may laugh, but they know that someone is hurt, so they feel unsafe around you when you do that. Let's think of ways you can use your ability with words and your sense of humor, maybe for your next writing assignment."

A student **gets very emotional** and calls another student names. The whole incident seems to have been blown out of proportion and you can't think of any positive element in it.

The student before you has emotional presence, a capacity or power that can be used for good or ill. If you want to see it used for good, you first acknowledge its existence. You might say, "Angela, one thing I notice about you that can be a strength in the future is that you have emotional presence. You are really *here* wherever you are. Whether you're feeling up or down, people know you're present and they can feel in touch with you because you have reserves of emotion that connect to them automatically. Good leaders often have this capacity and they guide it so that it helps others. You might not even notice the power of your feelings. Often when we're upset we can't tell how they affect others. What's not acceptable here is blame and anger toward others. If there's a problem between you and someone else, we want you to explain it to a teacher and then it's up to us what to do next. You can help by noticing a feeling starting to rise inside you. Usually you'll become very aware of it before you put words to it. So could you and I check a couple times a day about how feelings show up and how you handle them?"

A bright student tends to get the day's lesson quickly but then **spaces out** and draws pictures and ignores much of what occurs in class.

The negative is non-attention to the lesson, distracting others, and the model this provides to others to do the same. The positive is the student's quickness of mind and possible creative ability. Often keen thinkers are impelled to re-organize what comes to them so that they find it difficult to comply with routine. You might say, "Kevin, I appreciate about you that I can count on you to understand what I explain. You have a quick mind that will serve you well. But it misleads other students to see you divert from what we do in class. It leads others in that direction. Do you see the problem? We need to work out how to put your mind to work here at school. Maybe you can re-outline the lesson or go on to the next one, or we can arrange other things for you."

You first **identify** the root capacity being drawn upon and find in yourself genuine **respect** for it. To the student you identify it's **improper use** and the outcomes of this, project possibilities for its **positive use**, and address the **consequences** you contemplate. Following are more situations along with a couple sentences of a viewpoint to take. I assume that you're able to explain the negative outcomes of their behavior as in the examples above:

> A student fights: **"You're not afraid of physical encounters. You've evidently overcome fear of getting hurt."**

> A student criticizes others: **"You see that others could behave better. You see how they could improve."**

> A student bullies others, pushing them around: **"You have physical strength and assertiveness."**

A student comes late to everything: "You have your own clock, your own sense of timing and action."

A student ignores school rules, coming and going as she pleases: "You're able to be independent, to stand aside from usual rules."

A student lies: "A lie is a strategy for avoiding something unpleasant or gaining a benefit, at least for a time. You're able to design a strategy."

A student gathers a clique that rejects others: "You can make intense connections with a few people and are loyal to your friends."

A student is so quiet she never says anything: "You're very easy to get along with. You're a calming influence."

A student persists in negative behavior despite many attempts to get him to change: "You have strong persistence in following out your own idea. You're able to stick to something you want to do."

A student steals from another's locker: "You can make a plan and carry it out." If the action was instead impulsive, your comment might be, "You can see what looks like an opportunity and jump into it quickly. You're a quick responder."

A student is competitive and can't tolerate anyone else winning: "You have a drive to excel."

A student distracts the class with comic gestures and motions. "You can make people laugh."

This approach sustains our link with the student by conveying respect and avoiding words with negative implications or a critical tone. We're objective and straightforward, saying nothing a student must defend against. He doesn't wince from a subtle dig but instead receives accurate information pro and con about his action.

A fundamental balance makes the approach work. On the one hand, we gain credibility by accurately acknowledging the negative aspects of the student's behavior, which in turn makes our positive comments also believable. This practice can bridge even to students who seem to try deliberately to appear at their worst, and diminishes their desire to misbehave. Many wish desperately to be respected but feel driven to find out the truth of what others think of them. If their misdeed loosens a condemnation from a teacher, it was worth it to them to get into some trouble to find out. If, on the other hand, the teacher finds a basis of respect, they have a tiny purchase on a better view of themselves.

The approach doesn't change the subject. If we address a student's sarcasm, it's a diversion to say, "You're physically strong." Though true, it leaves hanging the question of what we think of his sarcasm. Search out the helpful shred within the objectionable behavior: "So you felt that he was backing you up" or "It made you feel strong for that time" or "You felt really original." We want access to their thinking about their behavior and gain it by finding a positive element and respecting it. As we need to, we say, "But do you see the flaw in that?" or "On the other hand, someone was injured, weren't they?" or "You excluded someone and hurt their feelings," or "You knew that was against school rules, right?"

If students respect you and exhibit a negative attitude in front of you, they invite you to draw on your best thoughts and grapple with their ideas. Those we most want to reach believe that something in them is so bad they can't even talk about it with a respectable person, so they reveal it in tangential behavior. Negativity they feel at first as a temporary state can gradually take over and pervade their moods permanently.

Think of their need to realize the good about themselves in light of what we know about juvenile corrections. The sheer time young people spend in that system correlates best with how much more crime they engage in later. The more "correction" they receive, the worse they get. How could this be? Certainly the worse their behavior, the longer their initial sentences. But the impact of this is that the longer an experience channels their thinking, the more completely it fills in a picture of themselves in society. If everywhere around them they see a maladaptive plan, when they select what to do, all they have to choose from are maladaptive plans!

So reminders of their strengths and even their small good intentions are important details in redesigning their picture. Their minds may be so oppressed by negative experience that they don't know how to be positive *even mentally* and must leave it to you where to place the key. If you can tease out a positive from what they say, they appreciate it. And as you deal objectively with it, they note that they're more likely to claim it by accepting your interpretation. This process, slow at first, accelerates as they feel better by applying the thinking you suggest.

With uncooperative behavior from several at once, your bottom line is to say with a wistful tone to your voice, "Well, perhaps you're not ready to get into this just today." The phrase "just today" implies that tomorrow may be different, that blocks are temporary. "We'll try again another time," you say, and take them into a challenging lesson or behavioral consequence (cf. 28. Use Consequences).

Often students' experience contains a valuable lesson, but they fail to notice and claim it. If they understand how they already meet their needs in acceptable ways, they're more likely to reuse the same means. A simple tool is passing on your observation of cause and effect in one-liners, summarizing briefly their behavior and its outcome:

You listened and felt connected.
You paid attention and got into the work easier.
You took a chance and had more fun.
You remembered and others valued that.
You thought it through and figured it out.

21. Study Feelings

Many programs offer ways to assist students' affective development. The need for addressing this zone is well understood (9). We'd like to make all students expert in the conscious management of it. Besides the means suggested in other sections, we note here a few that are simple and basic:

1. **Vocabulary.** We enter the internal zone by naming it accurately. A body of knowledge opens just by becoming familiar with its vocabulary.

    Pick out feelings you identify as important for your group or let students select them (cf. Appendix 1). Then just understand what each feeling means. Name one, ask a student to look it up and share the definition with the class, and invite anyone's experience with it. Ask them to watch for the feeling as the day unfolds (which prompts them to manage their feelings all day), and report later. You 1) identify a feeling, 2) offer a perspective on it, 3) ask them to note when it occurs, and 4) do a Consult at the day's end about their observations.

    They increase understanding by clustering feelings. To do so, they must think about the meaning of each one and the differences among them. Pick out twenty and ask pairs or teams to talk out how to group them as pleasant, unpleasant, brief, long-lasting, important, or unimportant; or by how they isolate or connect people or how they reflect positive or negative feelings about oneself. Doing this they're more likely to realize that they can choose to adopt many feelings consciously.

2. **Class discussion.** Class discussions about their personal concerns are a vehicle. The appendices offer many topics and your class can adapt and prioritize its own list. Note the progression of the questions below from general and impersonal to specific and immediate.

    What things generally give people good feelings (10)?
    Name all the ways students can give others good feelings.
    What does it mean to be a friend?
    How do people show they're friendly?
    How many friends can a person have?
    Are there different kinds of friends?
    How can people be kind and helpful at school?
    What things usually give you a good feeling?
    What things about school give you a good feeling?
    How do good feelings affect you differently than bad feelings?
    How does it affect you when people are friendly?

Name something you have at home that gives you a good feeling.
Tell about a time recently when someone gave you a good feeling.
How could I give you a good feeling?

3. **Assignments.** Analyze how historical events were impelled by emotions such as love, hate, greed, hubris, resentment, confidence, fear, and optimism. Embed the theme in assignments for writing and for interpreting current events.

4. **The Consult.** The Consult (accent the first syllable) helps you discover their prevailing mood, unify their focus, and initiate a discussion. Use it at the beginning of a period to gain their attention or following an outburst in class, a playground problem, a school event, a learning performance, a public calamity, or one person's experience that has meaning for others.

   Ask a question everyone can answer in a single word or phrase about the impact of the event. It may have provoked an emotional reaction, could be viewed from several angles, or reminded them of a personal experience. You might ask:

   What did you feel when (the event) happened?
   What are you feeling now about it?
   What thought came to your mind when the event happened?
   What do you think about it now?
   What word summarizes that experience for you?

   Wait briefly while everyone formulates their answer. Tell them you'll listen to each one before discussing them, and then invite their word, phrase, or sentence. Based on what you hear, engage them as you wish afterward (cf. Chapter 9 for how one incident was handled).

5. **Start the day.** Their habitual, subjective world comes face to face in the morning with the larger objective world the classroom represents. You might use a Consult then by saying, "Give one word about your current feeling." Notice if anyone shares a feeling that could hinder learning. Who's sad, discouraged, mad, upset, or tense? Respond with listening to the experience attached to the feeling, affirm an aspect of what the student shared, and understand how causes played out. If needed, problem-solve by talking out an action, making an appointment, or selecting a topic for later discussion. Knowing their place is secure, that they're affirmed, and that their problem is on the way to being managed, they can better address the current activity: 'Well then, is everyone ready to go to work?" If they have a feeling they don't want to expose to the class personally but would like it considered, let them suggest it privately to you as a topic for class discussion.

6. **Use unplanned experiences.** Use "targets of opportunity," unscheduled events begging for a response.

    One day my students went out for recess into moist snow, and a snowball fight erupted. Soon I noted unhappy expressions: aggrieved, vengeful, and defensive. Some believed that others had "ganged up" on them and some were observers. Several issues begged for resolution.

    A superb discussion followed in which the aggrieved stated their case, observers supplied information, those responsible for injury admitted their excesses and apologized, and the group together created guidelines that modified later snowball fights.

    Such experiences offer easy success: *Have your basket ready in case they shake the tree*. At some point during the year, an event may occur that touches everyone, and all have something they wish to relate—an action they observed or heard, a perception to verify, or a feeling to note—and all will be open to hearing from everyone else. If your class lives an untroubled existence, you may wish to plan an occasional group experience likely to test them a little, and generate the meaningful material deliberately. In either case, prepare your plan. *Carpe diem.*

7. **Affirmation activities.** Many activities approached with a sense of play can help even older students grasp the reality of their feelings: 1) Name a feeling or a common experience that evokes a feeling (e.g. petting your cat) and count how many students have had it. 2) How pleasant was it? (Little ones can raise their hand above ground to show how "high" the feeling was). 3) How intense? (Arms hugging self tightly or loosely). 4) How long in duration? (Arms extended little or much to either side, fingers pointing away.) 5) Cut out pictures from magazines and discuss what the person might be feeling. 6) If their name were a feeling, what would their name be? They make a nametag for themselves that expresses their feeling of the day and wear it. 7) Make a pie with each slice representing how much of a different feeling they carry around (usually, or right then). Change the size of the pieces as needed. 8) Search around inside. What do they find there? 9) Shift deliberately between three feelings. If they experience an unhappy one from time to time, they change it to an experience of feeling happy and then to one of feeling peaceful. With the negative experience, it's enough to sense the edge of the feeling without immersing themselves in it, and then move their attention to the positive ones. Notice how they change inside as they shift their focus from one to another. 10) Let's celebrate someone today. Be free to ask to be celebrated. 11)

Discuss what they can do if they think someone else gives them a bad feeling. Do they have to accept the gift?

8. **Go for it.** One teacher had an hour a week with middle school students assigned to her because of their problem behavior, and in a school year eliminated their problems. She moderated a discussion about issues in emotional self-management and exhibited superior communication skills herself, but she also expected them to absorb everything. She concluded each session by extending an invitation, "Okay, who's ready to *go for it?*" She'd invite one student to summarize the entire hour's discussion and incorporate every student's contribution. They all could do this, she said, a notable achievement in respect, attention, and remembering. It caused them to weigh their own words carefully, knowing someone would refer to them later, and absorb others' ideas better.

9. **Questions about feelings**. The questions below can help students connect one-to-one with others whom they either want to understand or aid. Have them learn the questions in order as a Learning Feat. Suggest that they ask them of someone outside the class and report what happens:

1   **What do you feel now?**
2   **Did the feeling come from inside or outside?**
3   **What happened to make you feel that?**
4   **Have you had the feeling before?**
5   **What happened then?**
6   **What else did you feel then?**
7   **What did you think then?**
8   **Have you tried to change it before?**
9   **How can you help change the feeling now?**
10 **What choices do you have?**
11 **How can I help?**

Once while I was observing a class, a student came up to me and rapidly asked me a half dozen of the questions above. I was startled at the sense of connection the exchange created. The questions elicit three critical themes: 1) the nature of one's feelings, 2) the sources of and associations with them, and 3) how one expects to manage them.

22. Breathe for Calming

We habitually take our breathing for granted as it goes in and out irregularly. To make it regular requires a conscious focus. The moment our attention wanders, the irregular rhythms resume.

Because of the continuous, deliberate attention required, breathing evenly in and out draws our mind away from its habitual worries and distractions, stabilizing the body and calming the mind. It also increases oxygen intake.

Just ask students to breathe at exactly the same rate for a few minutes. A gauge at their mouth or nose would record a constant rate of liters per minute of air passing that point in and out. Ask them to monitor their level of inner calm and assign it a 0-10 score with the latter the calmest. They'll notice their inner world becoming steadily more serene.

Quiet humming offers benefit also by significantly increasing the nitric oxide in the sinus cavities, reducing susceptibility to infection and increasing blood flow in the capillaries of the brain for numerous benefits to learning (11). Aid students further by asking them to close their eyes, sit erect and balanced to minimize body tension, and bring a single calming image before their mind.

Few activities you can ask of students for three to five minutes are as universally centering as these three done together—steady breathing, humming, and a calming image.

23. Understand Causality

We can think of students' energy as flowing in rivers, streams, and rivulets. Usually we can divert the rivulets with requests, consequences, and rewards. The rivers of their energy are so substantial, however, that they typically change only through personal insight and choice. Because emotions comprise much of this energy, we need to help students understand and direct them.

The micro-steps within an emotional experience are points when choice can be exerted, a kind of "feeling chain": 1) the pre-existing situation, 2) causes or triggers of the feeling, 3) its internal effects and sensations, 4) how the student handled it, and 5) the outcomes.

Begin by selecting a feeling important to your students, positive or negative. Choose it yourself (e.g. embarrassment) or help them do it (cf. Appendix 1). Write the feeling at the top center of the writing board, divide the board into five wide columns, and from the left title them "Situation," "Causes," "Effects," "Choices," and "Outcomes." Ask students to make a similar chart on a sheet of paper for their own study. Questions for each stage are below. Each question can elicit an insight though you may not have time for all of them. A few at each stage are enough to generate an overview you can refine later.

Invite one experience with the feeling from each of four to six students to track. They volunteer answers for you to summarize in brief words and phrases a column at a time, creating a sense of expanding a common frontier of knowledge. Place a student's comments about subsequent stages to the right of his or hers at an earlier one. As you work on the board with a few experiences, invite others to apply the template to themselves, filling in the columns on their personal sheet:

Situation. In this column jot their description of the situation just before the feeling was triggered.

Where were you (physical location)?

What were you expecting or wanting?

Was there a setup likely to produce the feeling?

Were you with people who influence you?

Was there a positive or negative feeling occurring already?

If so, was it strong or weak?

The key learning from this stage is that a setting can make a feeling more likely to happen, so choosing where they are is their first means of managing their feelings.

Causes. Here write what elicited or sparked the feeling.

What choices did you make just before the feeling came on?

What was the trigger that spurred the feeling, such as a word, deed, or event?

Did you foresee that this would happen?

Did you allow others to influence you?

Draw out how individuals react differently to the same trigger, and that they can choose to change how they receive it or can let it sail past them. A student might say about a negative feeling directed toward him/her, "I just think 'Cancel!' when I hear that." The key learning is that for external causes to affect them inwardly, they must consent. They can head off a feeling if they want to, which is the second point of leverage.

Effects. After they've reacted to the trigger and allowed the feeling to begin inside them, seemingly automatic impacts affect their mind and body.

What were your first reactions?

What did you do and say that seemed automatic?

What images and thoughts occurred?

What did they remind you of?

What feelings and body sensations came up?

How strong were the sensations and how long did they last?

Could you influence the strength of any feelings or sensations?

Did the event replay old feelings or experiences?

The key learning is that their prior choices can immerse them in an inner experience only partly under their control but they can expand or minimize its effect. They can catastrophize or place it in perspective, which is their third occasion for managing it.

Choices. Enter here the conscious behavioral choices they made to cope with or steer their experience after the feeling occurred and they noticed effects from it.

How deliberate were your choices?

At the time, did you think your choice was the right one?

How long did you think about what to do?

Did you consider long-term effects or just short-term?

Did you pause to think about others or just yourself?

What did you choose?

They decide to express, manage, or moderate their feeling, which is their fourth point of leverage for change.

Outcomes. Finally, note the results of the different ways students managed their experience:

Were the outcomes positive or negative? (Write a large + or - by experiences you tracked.)

What did you and others think, do, and feel?

If the feeling was negative, how did you get past it?

What did you learn?

What is your feeling now about the experience?

How do you wish you had handled it?

With this last look at their experience, their fifth occasion for exerting control, they rethink what they'll do next time in a similar situation.

The steps can bring a seemingly reflex response under their management. As they learn to foresee the progression of an event, they can choose whether to allow its steps to happen the way they're headed or to redirect them. Discussing the stages in small groups can deepen their understanding, and you might make up a handout for their personal use in understanding a recurrent feeling.

24. Self Correction

For any way we act unproductively, we have a set of thoughts propelling it. We change the action by changing the instructions we give ourselves.

Ask students to draw a line down the middle of a sheet of paper. Title the left column "Old" and the right one "New." On the left, ask them to list all their thoughts that come up repeatedly. You'd expect that the list would be endless, but there seems to be a practical maximum of a dozen, give or take a couple. These few comprise about 90% of our mental activity by recycling our central preoccupations, frustrations, hopes, and fears. Often they follow a recurrent feeling, so to help students discover them you can suggest "Notice the feelings you have often, and then pick out the thought that accompanies each feeling." Three-quarters or more of your own statements may be positive, like "I love my wife (husband)," or "My kids are great," while others focus on difficulties like "This co-worker really bugs me," or "How can I increase my income?", or "What am I going to do if X happens?"

It may take students time to compose their list. Start with ten minutes, set the list aside, and return to it later or the next day. As they reflect on their feelings in the past week, more thoughts usually come up. If they're nosy about what others write, tell everyone that you'll collect their pages, no one else will see them, and you'll hand them back when they work on them next.

When they've written ten or more, look at each one's list with them individually. They first identify the thoughts already positive and constructive, and write them in the "New" column to save as they are.

The remaining ones that aren't constructive contain the changes they need to make. Help them identify a replacement thought that addresses the same situation but is proactive, realistic, positive, and learning-oriented. For example, "I'm worried I'll fail the test" becomes "I get what I've prepared for. I can do better by working harder next time." The feeling of anxiety in the first idea changes to realism and determination. "Barbara is always teasing me and I hate it" turns into "I can ignore and release what people like Barbara do." Helplessness and frustration become detachment. "I can't wait till . . ." becomes "I can focus on what I'm doing now and time will pass faster." Longing becomes patience. An alternate idea applies a different emotional stance in the situation.

They write each improved thought in the New column, and compile all the ideas there into a fluid, connected paragraph, give it a title like My New Life, carry it with them always, and read it at least daily. When one of the old thoughts comes up, they're to take out the paragraph, read it thoughtfully, call up its optimism, determination, and realism, and deal with the situation from that viewpoint. The new viewpoint nudges them to call on their strengths instead of their weaknesses.

When they can't imagine any substitute for a negative thought, ask them to think of someone they know who could handle that situation smoothly, and what they might think as they did so. Read your student's old sentence, propose a better one, and ask, "Would this fit? Would this be a good replacement? Could you go to this one instead?"

Be sure to address exactly the same situation their old thought addresses. People often try to cope with a problem by turning their mind to something else, substituting an *unrelated* positive one for the negative thought. Although this is often appropriate, it may mean avoiding a problem instead of solving it. Thought patterns unaltered remain ready to sabotage.

25. Resource State

A resource state is a set of capacities we use to cope successfully, our constructive attitudes linked to our practical skills (12). Confronted with an angry co-worker, we reach for confidence that enables us to listen carefully and respond effectively. If we're criticized, we may need curiosity; if hurried, need balance and a sense of timing; if faced with loss, need acceptance and release. If we're blamed, we want the truthful, problem-solving part to come forward and not the angry, resentful part. For every situation we face, some part of us handles it better than another.

We can help students assemble a general resource state they can apply anytime. Say to them:

Today we're going to start on your resource state. We may take several days to finish it. I want you to think of experiences and memories that give you a feeling of strength or competence, as when you play a game and make a score. What's the feeling it gives you?

When students already feel good, their resource state is typically easy to access. They need it most just when it's hardest to obtain—when they're fearful, stressed, or unable to shake negative feelings. To prepare them for this, we first construct an internal state that's neurologically fused and then open an associative trail they can follow back into it. In a sense, they become able to open a series of inward doors from one perception to another, quickly remember their competence and confidence, and bypass their maladaptive reactions.

Brainstorm with them a list of productive, positive, personal *actions* that give them good feelings about themselves. When did they show competence, understanding of others, determination, confidence, insight, or other abilities? Give a name to their experience and note the trait associated with it. The word "accident" could refer to a time when they rose to an occasion, knew what to do, and felt confident. "Game" might remind them of a sports event when they felt successful. When everyone has several, ask them to choose the five or six that most completely represent the resources they'd want to call on again.

Your next step is to join such fragments of feeling and self-image into a unified sense of themselves. Do it by three cues or reminders that are under their control—a word, an image, and a gesture. Performed together they embed in their physical body a switch which, when thrown, turns on their strengths. The trail opens readily to them if they follow it several times in situations of increasing challenge.

Instruct them to *select a key word* that unifies all of their resource experiences, such as the one designating an experience they liked, or just an overall word like "confidence." A woman I worked with used the word "climbing" to remind her of how resourceful she felt after an experience of rock-climbing. Select also *an image* that appeals to them. It may be of themselves doing a challenging action; or a physical object, person, or location that gives them a lift, or a symbol they invent. Finally, select *a gesture* like the "okay" symbol with thumb and forefinger in a circle. They are to use these three together—the word, image, and gesture—solely when they want to remind their brain to re-find and call up the resource state they want. They avoid using the combination unless that's specifically what they intend to do.

When all have named at least five resources and have selected their three cues, have them sit quietly, close their eyes, and imagine deeply and vividly the first resource on their list. *They call up the feelings they enjoyed when it first occurred.* That's the crucial step, access to the feeling of it. Ask them to nod their heads silently when they've gained it. When all are in touch with it, ask them to say their key word, bring their key image before their mind, perform their gesture, and enjoy the good feeling for a minute. Do this with each resource separately, and then run through the entire list two or three times until they can just "fire" the three cues and re-experience the good feeling from each resource. This unites the resources into a common state.

For a few minutes during each of the next several days, ask them to calm themselves, go within, and return to their resource state using the three cues (and reliving the positive memories as needed). Even brief practice can make them more secure in restoring their resource state when they need it. Note any who may need extra practice with you.

If some say "I don't have any experiences that are resources for me," direct their attention *to feelings they generate from their own actions:* "The best feelings we get come from what we ourselves do. Can you give someone else a good feeling? What needs can you meet? What abilities do you have that are satisfying whenever you do them?" Survey their age-appropriate competences. You may start some off with positive feedback: "Now close your eyes, listen carefully, and notice what happens inside you when I say something." When they're ready, pay them a sincere compliment about a strength they have. The resource they acknowledge is already theirs, but they may grasp it better when you put it into words. Ask them if they notice a change inside as they receive what you say. If they do, tell them, "Well then, we can make that one of your resources. That's what resource states do. We create our resource state just from the things that give us good feelings about ourselves." Appreciation Time and the CSCS point them to many gestures of consideration they can exhibit that are likely to be acknowledged quickly, generating better feelings. Suggest behaviors they can try out, and ask them check with you daily until they have five they can assemble into a unified resource state.

26. Life Knowledge

As we raise children, we often override their thoughts, feelings, and desires with what we believe is better for them. As they expand their understanding, we apply this to ideas. Our use of "should" essentially says "You need to set aside what you believe, feel, or think about this. Do it my way." We substitute our thought processes for theirs to get the conclusion we want, which keeps them safe while they slowly assimilate adult thinking. For a middle school student, the thought "My parents will kill me if I do that" may be enough for the time being.

To prepare them for the adult world, however, we enlist their understanding of reality. We want their own perceptions to lead them to the best thing whether their significant elder told them so or not. For this, they need to examine the world instead of merely what we want of them. We look at the world together with them, and invite them to master solutions to the practical (and moral, relational, familial, economic, and academic) problems it presents: "If you want to be successful later, carve this idea into your brain so you can use it when you need it."

Such knowledge can include all kinds of good advice. Form as question and answer any idea that strikes you as true and important, have them write it in their Miscellaneous notebook section, and score it on the scoreboard as a Learning Feat. With but occasional time spent, you can help them absorb guidelines they'll apply for life. Here are some ways to work with the ideas below:

With older students, present just the questions to research and think out.

Incorporate the answers below unless theirs are superior.

Apply the ideas to experiences they have.

Compare different people's views about the answers.

Use them as topics for Total Attention talking time and small group discussion.

Model the answers yourself.

Explain how they might have been used during events students know of. The questions vary in complexity but all deserve integration into students' habitual thinking.

1   *How do I gain control of my life?*
     Make a promise to myself in a small area.
     Keep the promise.
     Extend that to more areas.

2   *How long will adults run my life?*
     Until I consistently make wise judgments on my own.

3   *What are two basic laws at the foundation of our legal system?*
     Do all that you agree to do.

Do not encroach on other persons or their property (13).

4   *When you disagree with someone, what's the first thing to do?*
Try to understand their point of view.

5   *What are two questions to ask yourself as you work with others?*
How can I help you?
What can I learn from you (14)?

6   *What strengthens your motivation to change?*
Having reasons you care about.

7   *What trait makes the biggest difference between success and failure?*
Persistence.

8   *What is the first step to giving others good feelings?*
To *want* them to feel good.

9   *What's the main way people become irrational?*
They see the world only through their own experience.

10   *Name the skills that help most in school.*
Listen well.
Give others good feelings.
Remember.

11   *How do you become skillful at anything?*
Find out what effort pays off.
Practice the effort

12   *What is the hardest but most important thing to do in communications?*
Maintain good communications with others when you're having intense feelings yourself.

13   *What's the first thing to do if you don't like how others treat you?*
Notice how you treat them.

14   *How can we help ourselves out of pain and hurt?*
Recognize that they freeze the mind into mediocre thinking.
Find safe people to be with.
Release the pain and hurt.

15   *How do I set standards for myself?*
Go beyond what others expect of me.

16   *What are four keys to concentration?*
Goal: Know what you want to accomplish.
Means: Know where to put your attention in order to achieve it.
Focus: Ignore everything else while you do that.
Persistence: Keep at it until you reach your goal

Roots of behavior. Students need alternatives to their dysfunctional ideas. If a student is sneaky or evasive, you face him privately, point out the unsatisfactory behavior, let your firm caring convey "I'm concerned about this for you," and focus on the belief he employs. Maybe his distorted ideas will be a future problem if he doesn't change them.

Many principles that structure civilized life deserve extended class discussions. A range of helpful formats are available in commercially marketed programs, but just by enlisting your students in a search for ideas that are both true and important, you can generate much positive thought. Note the questions boxed here. They invite knowledge instead of opinion. Planting students' minds in a common, substantial reality is the best basis upon which they can re-think what they do. When views are opposed, you help them focus on the accurate appreciation of each: "If everyone believed this, how would it affect society?" This isn't conveying an ideology but rather helping them make sense of what they perceive. Rehabilitation programs in some way must confront the ideas from which

> **What is a neighbor?**
> **What are rights?**
> **What is a law?**
> **What is responsibility?**
> **What is an agreement?**
> **What is a contract?**
> **What is encroachment?**
> **What is ownership?**
> **What is a truth?**
> **What is real?**
> **What is good?**
> **What is a belief?**
> **What is justice?**
> **What is freedom?**
> **What is a mistake?**
> **What is government?**
> **What is a family?**
> **What is integrity?**
> **What is discipline?**
> **What are cause and effect?**
> **What is a model?**

offenders select reasons for their behavior, and teach appropriate thinking. Any of us can remember when we had to acknowledge grudgingly that our thinking was incorrect even though our behavior continued to be resistant.

A helpful clue for assisting this change in them is that behavior is driven most *by the first idea that comes to our mind* in a given situation, usually the one to which we've most recently given energy. So when students learn a guideline and have the opportunity to apply it at once in class, they're likely to do so and then to use it again later (15). We tell them, "You need to know *how* to do this when it's called for. To apply good thinking outside class, you need to understand how inside class." Emotional satisfaction meshed with practical learning strengthens the unconscious presumption that they'll apply it. The pleasant aura and a memory of its usefulness established in class appeal to them later.

By discussing the questions boxed here, we show them that people examine their experience, accumulate ideas about it, and use their best thinking; and that they themselves can grasp and respond to what we say. In sum, *credible people embody and convey sensible ideas which students can verify from observation of reality and then apply, and for which they receive affirmation.* Any of these conditions missing weakens the effort.

Structure of thought. While many ideas about life and society can be valuable, only a scant handful typically guide any one person. So if we can expand their claim on specific ones that are useful, the better the odds that they'll draw on them later. Mental competence can be thought of as the range of perspectives the mind can bring to bear on an issue. Those below comprise a tool kit for intellectual flexibility. Photocopy them for everyone, explain them, and apply them to students' experience:

1. **CAUSE-EFFECT. What determines or affects what, both obvious and subtle?**
2. **CERTAINTY. What is absolutely certain and what's uncertain?**
3. **COMFORT. How do people's comfort and pleasure affect this?**
4. **COMPARE-CONTRAST. How is this the same as or different from something else?**
5. **EVENTS. Was this a specific happening or ongoing? Does it relate to other events past, present, or future?**
6. **FACT. Is this fact or opinion, an issue resolved by data or interpretation?**
7. **IMPORTANCE. What scale of importance should be used to judge this? What values are represented?**
8. **MATERIALS. What are the physical components or parts? What is seen, heard, shaped, formed, or handled?**
9. **MEANING. 1) What did the author say? (Quote his/her words.) 2) What did the author mean? (Use the author's other writings.) 3) What do you understand it to mean? (Draw on other knowledge you have.) 4) How do you use or apply it?**
10. **MOTIVATION. What purpose or intent moved those who brought this about? What influences were major and minor?**
11. **PART-WHOLE. How is this part of something larger? What are its parts?**
12. **PATTERN. How is this ordered or patterned? How is it free, formless, or changing?**
13. **PEOPLE. Who is affected? Who participates? Who benefits?**
14. **PRINCIPLES. What are the governing ideas, the form given to major thoughts?**
15. **PROCESS. Is this a "how to do" something, a sequence of orderly activity?**
16. **REASONS. Is this evidence that supports something else? Does it stack up logically?**
17. **RULES. Is this a rule for understanding or doing something?**

18 **SUBJECTIVE-OBJECTIVE. Does this exist mainly in someone's mind as their view of the world, or does it exist in external reality?**
19 **SUBSTANCE-QUALITY. What is the basic nature, the thing in itself? What are the characteristics of this basic nature?**
20 **VISIBILITY. Is this obscure, concealed, or obvious? Are appearances different from truth? Are there layers of meaning?**

Add to the list any factor you want them to think about as they approach new knowledge or situations. The principles are razors for sifting meaning. Sciences use cause/effect, part/whole, facts, and certainty. Literature draws on subjective/objective, purpose, people, principles, and qualities. Politics, government, and history are affected greatly by comfort, motivation, events, process, rules, and visibility. As you present a subject, explain how a given factor applies. Ask them to analyze their reading and assignments in terms of it, build it into the explorations you direct, and apply it to new viewpoints they encounter.

At some point in their learning, students need to understand the intellectual and moral effort involved in finding truth (concordance between symbol and symbolized).

The most common offense against truth is that people pride themselves on asserting the rightness of what they knew before instead of taking pleasure in grasping possible correction. One of my professors, who'd authored a two-volume set of history books, was asked by a student what he'd come to believe was the most difficult virtue to practice. He replied, "Intellectual honesty." Without it, all other problems get worse. We all face an obligation to welcome correction, counteract our desire to please ourselves, and restrain our mind from bending information. You model this by how you modify your own ideas based on new information, and thank them when they correct you. Only conscious effort purifies our description of reality so it's undistorted.

27. Guide Behavior

The secret of success is strenuous limitation, an editorial writer declared in one of my father's trade journals. People focus their energy like a powerhouse confines a flow of water to generate electricity, he explained. We can apply this idea to the classroom in several ways:

Create experience of manner. With students we attempt to do something similar to what powerhouses do with water. We'd like to channel a cerebral exercise into a whole body-mind experience involving their entire lives if we could, but we face limitations. The past, future, abstract, and elsewhere aren't available to direct experience.

We remedy this deficit as best we can by eliciting physical activity in the *manner* of learning such as by research, projects, observation, note-taking, structuring, diagramming, writing, summarizing, rating, explaining to a partner, working in groups, and performing to the class.

Prepare behavioral choices. We can manage their behavior while they're in the classroom, but want them to act later on their own. Many issues they'll face will be hard, and we want them versatile enough to choose the disciplined effort needed then. We make this more likely by building it into their behavior now. Think of sports' contests, energy moving along clear channels to produce signs of success. We break the desired behavior into steps, and they learn, practice, and apply the steps. In the classroom we prepare their confidence that they can do hard things on their own. In a muted way we apply an idea expressed by Napoleon Bonaparte. Asked why he drove his army so hard, he replied "If you make everything hard, then the truly hard things become easy." Only the discipline to acquire a prior competence supplies the competence when it's needed.

Check misbehavior by correcting small things. A change in police attention in New York City improved public safety by focusing on small things. Checking minor misbehaviors communicated that they matter. People getting away with vandalism, graffiti, and misdemeanors sets a climate of lawbreaking and lack of caring. If society's representatives are indifferent to negative behavior, its orbit reasonably expands as people push the limits (16). This applies in schools. We focus their thinking and require their behavior in small things that we want them to apply more extensively later.

Teach values by behavior. We teach many critical social principles by redirecting behavior. We say to them, "Do this and here's why." If we instruct them that they should treat each other kindly, for instance, but ignore it when one child hurts another, they receive contradictory information. If no consequence occurs at school, the student is led to believe that no consequence occurs in life. If a student learns enough to graduate but his hurting others is passed over, he connects the dots: *As long as I do what's officially required, how I treat others doesn't matter.* Schools may unwittingly instruct students that getting answers right is more important than whether or not they injure others, a guideline that can't fail to bring unhappiness.

Remedy confusion by directing behavior. A continuum of behavioral shaping begins in kindergarten with lining up to go in and out. When schools expect children to run for the exits upon hearing an alarm, they emerge from the doors in a scattered mass. Their guideline might be phrased, "Save yourself." But if an emergency occurs, such a rule may work poorly because people can be trapped or injured. A better message might be, "Account for everyone," such as by assigning students to partners or triads that check on each other as they exit. Then run an impromptu drill. Give a dozen children secret instructions like, "Fell and broke my ankle," "Confused about direction," "Was scared to go out of the room," "Didn't want to stop what I was doing," "Needed to go to bathroom badly," and see how others account for their whereabouts. If checking on each other's well-being takes a few seconds longer, weigh the time lost against the gain in responsibility.

At the start of World War II when Alaska was invaded, I was a kindergartner there. In an air raid drill, we lined up, trooped out of the school, and hiked a short distance into the underbrush on the hillside above the school. In the event of an air attack, my row was assigned to crouch under a designated alder.

How to persist till a task is completed
How to prioritize
How to admit a mistake and apologize
How to receive correction gracefully
How to listen
How to work out a conflict
How to be a partner or teammate
What to do in an emergency
How to encourage someone else
How to help others be successful

The meaning of the drill was 1) adults have a plan, 2) I have a place in the plan, and 3) I'm taken care of if I cooperate. Forming a line and exiting the building expressed the life lesson that collective order gets us through emergencies. Adults cope constantly with daily experience through group patterns, so practicing some of them arbitrarily at school is not an inappropriate preparation for life. The goal isn't just their obedience to our orders but for them to realize how their behavior connects them to the group in which they survive.

Practice behavioral skills. If we want our lessons to make a difference, we have to root them in what we ask students to do, especially as we offer them action templates for situations likely to occur outside our guidance. When you know what you want them to do later, explain *how* (i.e. the internal perceptions and thoughts they'll carry out), and then do them in school while surrounding them with good feelings. Patterns like those boxed here need to be learned thoroughly so they're accessible resources. Add those you find useful in your own life, arrange for students to learn them, and provide a rationale for applying them.

28. Use Consequences

Human love shows up in your caring, your concern for children, and how you take pleasure in meeting their needs and making them successful. Caring isn't just your positive feelings. You meet needs by disciplining yourself to attend to what's best for them, overcoming any feeling-based variability in yourself. Character, as the saying goes, is what you do in spite of your moods. From within your personal field of self-discipline and respect, *your* actions need to elicit *their* actions.

Here we look at altering their unacceptable behavior through your actions of 1) being clear and firm, 2) using behavior instead of feelings as a signal for change, 3) causing students the minimum discomfort required to redirect them, 4) exerting a continuum of impact on them, 5) applying consequences for distraction, and 6) awarding Bonus Time.

Clear and firm. Rules are part of a system enabling students to learn with others. When rules are clear, you can administer consequences decisively while remaining positive and barely hesitating in the lesson (17).

Although your rules may be clear, the consequences of breaking them may not be, which can help you. You want students thinking "If I misbehave, things could get a whole lot worse." There's a saying in the Middle East, "If you know the ransom of your hostage, kill him." That is, if you know the effect of your behavior and can accept it, you can do what you please. Students may estimate that a misbehavior is worth the price of a known, minimal consequence they'll endure for it, so you may wish to leave open the sanction you'll apply.

"Firm" describes a boundary on their behavior, not your trait of rigidity. You sustain a limitation despite pressure against it, upholding a standard even against opposition. Many find this difficult to do. "Dad, they just tear the subs apart," my son commented about his high school classes one day. Students not even in the class would stroll in, act as though they belonged, give a false name, talk as they pleased, and entertain themselves at the teacher's expense. "Some subs come in, though, and from the minute they open their mouth, you know you can't mess with them," he continued. "They'll let you go so far and no farther." If you happen to have soft boundaries, notice whether they're getting you the classroom experience you want.

Behaviors versus feelings as signal. With some students, adult anger is a code. They hear, "Pay attention! Danger!" and listen intently until it passes. Because of the brief gain in their attention, you may resort to anger to manage them when clarity and firmness are enough. If you use your unhappiness as the *signal* that you demand a behavior change, they may wait for it before changing. Then, for you to manage the classroom, you can spend hours a day on the edge of unhappiness. You guarantee that they will "make" you that way if that's when they impact you strongly enough for you to require them to change. You set it up that way.

This is significant for their later life. They need to size up actual conditions for an early rather than a late signal to change their behavior, or they may go through life wondering "Why are people always angry at me?" In class, you want them to notice that a specific behavior triggers a predictable, impersonal rule that you administer while staying inside your own good feelings. Once you set up a standard that brings about a return to classroom attention, you needn't feel even hesitant about applying it—even though regretfully, because you'd prefer not to have to cause them discomfort.

Create discomfort. Classroom progress depends on having students' attention. We may correct individuals to obtain it, but when that isn't enough, uncomfortable consequences are our next step. Behavior is governed by its perceived benefit or loss, which provides us a guideline:

DISCOMFORT TODAY =
COOPERATION TOMORROW

Discomfort doesn't imply unhappy or negative feelings but just a motivating condition, like wanting to remove a rock in your shoe. In the opening scene of the movie *Patton,* General George S. Patton, commander of the Third Army during the World War II invasion of Europe, speaks to the troops of his command: "Your mission is not to go and give your life for your country. Your mission is to make your enemy give *his* life for *his* country." I refer to this as The Patton Principle: *Cause discomfort in your students rather than allowing them to cause discomfort in you.* Keep your own good feelings while administering discipline, and be unswayed by attempts to manipulate your rules or feelings.

Observe whether the consequences you apply cause the change you want. Sometimes they don't touch the motives for the misbehavior. Students may be glad to be sent out of class, go to the principal's office, or remain after school because they'd rather not go home anyway.

A continuum of impact. Arrange your options by their intensity of impact and use the least intense that works. Focus students on the lesson effectively, for instance, and all other issues diminish. Meet their emotional needs with constructive behavior and they're less likely to meet them destructively. Assuming you do so by the means described above, you also have a hierarchy of personal impact to draw on:

Start with *a look*: You glance at the student. He meets your eye, recognizes your message, and adjusts.

Stronger is *a longer look*. It communicates, "I notice what you're doing, it's unacceptable, and I'm going to keep on you till you change." It need not be a glare but just a look. The message is delivered and the student adjusts.

If the student still doesn't change, *you increase the impact* and so must understand what constitutes the next increment in this class for this student.

It often lies *in approaching and facing*. You bring your longer look closer, limiting the student's behavior neutrally. You calm yourself and face the student at the same eye level. The most powerful word you can use is the student's name: "Charles." Your tone implies a positive motive. "Do you need something, perhaps?" If a car ran over his dog or his parents just announced their divorce, you'd like to know. "Could we make an adjustment here?" or "Can I help you with something?"

Next in the sequence is *a description of the unacceptable behavior*. This is not blame, threat, nor even a request for a change, but conveys information gently and evenly: "Jennifer, you're talking while Aaron is giving his answer," a positive message rather than a rebuke. It conveys, "You may not realize the impact you have right now, and just knowing about it you might want to make an adjustment."

Following that is *a direct request for the behavior you want*. You have a choice of words to speak in a personal tone, one human being to another. Communicate what you want the student to do in words you'd be glad to have him/her imitate later (your modeling, of course, works every minute of classroom time): "I'd appreciate it if . . . ," or "It's your turn," or "It's hard to listen to two people at the same time," or "Please follow what's on the board now."

You may need to *explore motivation*. Assume that their behavior poses a question and find out what it is: "Are you trying to find a way to get things done? Get your viewpoint out? Lift your mood? Be helpful to the class? Change your feeling?" You may notice rhythmic tapping or eruptions telling you that energy is not linked to the classroom task. Cynical words and attitudes may need challenging: "Let me explain what we're trying to do here."

Focus on the desired behavior rather than the undesired. An unconscious mechanism responds in an unexpected way to negative commands like "Stop making noise!" or "Stop interrupting!" or "Stop snickering!" If you find yourself using the word "Stop!" frequently, it's critical that you *find a new strategy*. Note the form of that phrase, *find a new strategy*. The action it pictures is different from what you were doing before. You weren't "finding a new strategy" a minute ago, so I'm inserting a different instructional CD into your internal computer, so to speak. If instead I'd written " . . . *it's critical that you stop doing that,*" what imagery do I leave? There's no change. "Doing that" is still the image even though it has an X through it.

A useful understanding about the unconscious is that it doesn't process well our grammatical niceties that X out what we don't want, our ways to say no. It prefers the big nouns and verbs, the images. When it hears "making noise," "interrupting," and "snickering," it converts them to commands: "I guess that's what I'm supposed to do." Many years ago, Philip Morris cigarettes promoted "Less Irritation." When sales dropped nationwide, the company asked smokers what came to mind when they thought of Philip Morris. Their answer? "Irritation." The word "less" didn't reverse the negative imagery implied in the other word.

You might also elicit information, remind the student of an agreement, or request a conference. Be clear and brief in speaking, and stay face to face silently until you receive a nod. Notice which of you blinks first, which is an unconscious signal of deferring to the other. Staying "inside his space" makes it difficult for him to dismiss you. When he senses that you won't back down, he typically adjusts.

For more serious behavior, you have parent conferences, making a plan, suspension, time-out, in-school detention, after-school detention, a talk with the principal, time with the counselor, and finally transfer to a facility designed to manage the behavior. Use the minimum intervention that obtains what you want. Extreme sanctions can invite manipulation, give reason for rebellion, and incline you to relax a rule.

Consequences for Distraction Time. The value students place on freedom makes possible a fine-tuned consequence that operates early in the spectrum of misbehavior. It has logical consistency, a one minute loss of freedom for one minute of distraction.

I assume here that you can either hold students after class time or can require them to return at another time. If you can do so, even keeping them one extra minute immediately after the bell has an impact because there's a distended sense of urgency when they're poised to leave. Your steps are:

1   **Obtain a timer with a second-denominated stopwatch function.**
2   **Explain to students that whenever someone doesn't respond to your request for attention, you'll say, "Class!" and wait five seconds. Count "one elephant, two elephants" up to five in which they can complete their sentences, return to their seats, and face you (three checkable behaviors). Elementary classes might help you select a daily timing phrase that takes a second to repeat, such as from current events (one indictment, two indictments . . .) or from science (one Bernoulli, two Bernoullis . . .).**
3   **If they're not quiet in five seconds, raise the stopwatch where they can see it and press it to begin. When they're attentive, press it to stop. Save what's on it and add to it as needed later.**
4   **At the end of the period or day, ask them to put their books away and sit quietly after the bell for the total accumulated on the timer. The discomfort is minor but enough to spur one to whisper to another, "Hey, cut it out. Time is starting."**

You want them to value time more highly by using up time they value. By setting aside anything that could interest them, you help them savor its slow passage. You focus them solely on the loss of time they regard as theirs after they've been careless with time they regard as yours. You might grasp the impact of this when you're headed out the door late for an appointment while juggling a briefcase, a sandwich, and a cup of coffee, and your cell phone rings with a call you have to take. While you answer, check your watch also and feel how long it takes for a minute to pass. For some students, the discomfort of waiting while the seconds tick off is like a near-death experience, while others are just uncomfortable enough to pay better attention tomorrow.

Classes may react differently to the timer. A group of independent high school students introduced to it mid-year were restive. One confided to me that they were discussing how to "stuff the timer down the teacher's throat" but in a class meeting worked out satisfactory modifications. Try to set it up at the beginning of the year as but one feature of a system that includes interesting learning activities and an opportunity to earn free time.

Students may object that everyone shouldn't suffer for the behavior of a few. You can agree if you wish and apply consequences only to misbehaving students, but it divides the class and interferes with the cohesion you want. You might say this instead:

It's too complicated for me to keep track of how much time individuals distract the class. We're all in this together. Even one person distracting affects everyone. Most of the time, you can just remind someone near you that I'm asking for attention. When I say 'Class' and others don't notice, just point it out to them.

Besides ignoring you when you ask for their attention, some may disrupt an ongoing activity. Hold up the timer silently for a few seconds as a reminder and then time them until the disruption ceases.

Bonus Time. The Silver Bullet design implements fully the four intrinsic motives for learning proposed by Bruner. Students experience reciprocity in paired and group work, identification as they team up with others they respect, curiosity as they're freed to explore an expanded curriculum, and competence as their successes are demonstrated, scored, posted and celebrated.

To reinforce them further, *try something and watch carefully*. For many activities, they need only a stimulus—a word from us or a classmate, applause, a time appearing on the clock, the completion of a particular activity, a checkoff on a rating scale, a score appearing, and so on. Each stimulus should mark a success, that an equivalence has occurred between their effort and what they receive back. Grasping this equivalence accurately is critical. A librarian described to me a boy who'd been in and out of trouble. One day he checked out a stack of books and said to her hopefully, "I'm really going to try hard." My heart went out to him because he had no understanding of *the effort that would turn things around* and this was his best guess.

To try Bonus Time, discuss with students a collective benefit they'd like to work toward. Within your classroom they might want to watch a video for entertainment, play games, have free time, do something creative together, or accumulate time for a larger class purpose. Some settings may allow you to access outside resources like audio/visual or sports equipment, or computers.

A way to accumulate the time is to reward minute for minute their high-value observable behavior such as a student doing Impromptu Performance or a group doing Perfect Conversation. At the end of a day, for example, a randomly selected student stands and is asked all the questions from the day's work. The time of his or her performed answers earns equal time for the whole class. Or a small group carries out all the Perfect Conversation skills and you match their "perfect" talking time with reward time up to any cap you place on it. For managing distractions, you can assign them a presumptive hourly bonus of five minutes, and then reduce it a minute for each minute they divert the class (and increase it as they accomplish deeds you specify).

Making a **game of Bonus Time** can encourage them to maintain the prior month's learning. It works the way a player's score benefits a team, and draws on two aspects of the Silver Bullet design. Questions and answers are already organized and summarized in their notebooks, and the quantities of the answers are timed (or counted) and initialed by a listener. To create the game, 1) date new questions in students' notebooks when they first learn them. 2) When you wish to play the game, draw a student's name at random. 3) They hand you their notebook and you ask the questions from the prior day's work. 4) Time the answers, and add the amount to the class reward time up to any cap you place on it. Adding five minutes a day, students earn a bonus period in ten days. 5) With the questions numbered and dated, you can also draw a random time period from which to ask the questions. Drop tokens into a bag for Yesterday, Five Days, Ten Days, Twenty Days, and Thirty Days (i.e. the same day of the week for the past several weeks). Draw a token, count back that number of school days on the calendar, find the questions from that date in the student's notes, and ask them (using the following days' questions if needed to fill out the time). 6) Take the reward time off when it's convenient.

CHAPTER 5

Practice Learning

To adapt "practice makes perfect" to the classroom, we look at what comprises practice of knowledge and makes it effective, and how to apply it to numbers; with knowledge of varying exactness, small amounts of time, and beginning students; in conversation outside school and with methods that lead to perfect recall.

29. Peg List

The mind's natural way to counteract forgetting is to wait a moment and recall. A fresh impression is easiest to build on. A few glances at what just occurred are often sufficient to hold it. When we're running errands, meet a family friend, and converse a bit, we easily remember it so we can tell others at home. Thinking about it briefly restores our memory, and we relate the conversation in detail later.

In school, instead of providing a few later glances to maintain recent ideas, we constantly override them. We load students' wheelbarrow and then make them dump it so we can load it again. With most of what we present, they must start over even to begin its installation, wasting the first imprint we made in their short-term memory.

One day I discovered an easy alternative. After a couple of hours of concentration, I needed a change of pace. Thinking just to use my mind in a different way, I went to my shelf and picked out a book on Roman history, cracked it at random, and found myself immersed in the Roman civil war. Sulla's army raced to defend Rome from opposing forces and defeated them. Sulla then ordered his troops to butcher his captured foes in earshot of his conference with the Senate. After reading a page, I felt a shift in my attention, returned to my desk, set a timer for five minutes, and resumed my work.

Clear, firm
Behavior signal
Create discomfort
Continuum of impact
Time loss
Bonus time
B T game
Peg list
Sulla
wait, recall

The timer went off after what seemed but a moment. I stopped what I was doing, turned my mind back to Rome, and without reviewing the pages could remember the scenes vividly. Later I did the same with a page from a book on organizational development. Again five minutes later, the knowledge stood ready in my memory. On a small slip of paper on my desk, I noted "Sulla" and "organiz/problem-solving," and on following days added other words to the list about current events, personal incidents, research, and reading. A brief daily mental review of the list, often just while driving, was enough to retain the substance of most of the ideas. The list gradually became an ongoing index of everything I wanted to save for active thought, a birds-eye view of interesting ideas I'd run across. I called it "a peg list," using one word to peg a larger idea. Note the box nearby that illustrates. Perhaps you can recall what the words refer to from the prior section, or easily recover their meaning with a glance. They're a memory hook and not an outline. You hold the terms in mind only long enough to recall their main meaning.

Such brief but focused time spent in input/output can enable students to save enormous amounts of knowledge. You can identify the points yourself or leave their selection to students: "We have fifteen minutes left in the period. Please read your history book for items for your Peg List." Or a student jots down six ideas during math class and then begins social studies. He takes a few seconds interspersed through that period to recheck the images from math. By the end of the day, he's re-noted the ideas on his list a dozen times each, sinking them deeply into memory with little added time and effort.

Pegs can match points in Learning Feats and offer topics for Impromptu Performance. To track individual ideas to a reference, students can note a page number with the peg.

30. The Practice Element

The practice element is the degree to which students draw on an existing internal model of their knowledge. The Peg List just explained is one way to do this, and tests are a common example. Students must supply some aspect of knowledge from their own store of it. To prepare for a test, they practice what they can draw out of themselves. The more pieces they already have inside, the more they can express. We can distinguish three levels.

Low. In activities with a low practice element, students are passive, needing no prior internal model. Knowledge comes to them from *outside* their own mind. The teacher may lecture while they take notes. They may read, watch videos or movies, listen to audiotapes or to other students answering questions, or ask questions of the teacher. Silent seat work may focus them on recognition, matching, linking, filling in blanks, or copying. These activities need little attention to carry out, don't depend on knowledge mastered before, and by themselves don't install it. They're most useful for drawing together a model of the knowledge that later effort deepens.

Medium. With these activities, some knowledge begins outside the student and some inside, but the student does call up an internal model to develop further.

Students can help each other correct errors, prioritize ideas, select the most important aspects to work on, offer analogies and ways to remember, convert information to questions and answers, summarize in writing, re-organize notes, have experiences and do experiments, and analyze with a new viewpoint something already learned. Writing helps to solidify the inner form of the knowledge at this level and to confirm meanings that otherwise remain vague. Students learn steadily as they spend time in the medium practice element.

High. With a high practice element, the student *already possesses all pieces of knowledge,* so that drawing on them reinforces the inner model most fully. Students answer questions, explain their knowledge to a listener without help, debate issues about the subject, take tests, write without using prior notes, do any medium practice element with material drawn entirely from memory, or employ Silver Bullet methods like Impromptu Performance, Mental Movie, Walk Away, and Time Capsule. To make learning permanent, arrange for them to spend as much time as possible in high practice element activities. With anything we want them to save, we ask them to output answers until they're mastered.

Larson's design for increasing college students' learning applied the latter two levels, and should be suitable for senior high. Students paired up and studied two pages of text at a time. Then without looking at notes or diagrams, the recaller summarized the pages as completely as possible. The listener corrected errors and misunderstandings, noted omissions, and helped create novel ways of recalling the information. Recaller and listener switched roles every two pages and worked steadily through a part in one sitting. They clarified what they learned from each other and how they could improve their use of time, and helped each other by judging importance, elaborating on each other's summaries with images and analogies, and personalizing the material. Efforts at summarizing improved retention (18).

31. Designated Listener

An anxious, awkward, ill-dressed little girl from a large family happened to live at the end of a rural school bus route driven by Mary Dee, a warm and friendly person and a relative of mine. The two had a few minutes of private time going and coming every day to talk. After twelve years, when the girl graduated a confident person, she told Mary Dee with great feeling that their conversations a few minutes a day were the difference that enabled her to "make it."

Everyone deserves someone who will listen to them daily and unfailingly. To arrange this, designate a listener for every child. In class they do this to practice their learning, but a different impact occurs when someone outside the classroom waits eagerly to hear their new knowledge. If parents are busy, look for a sibling, older student, senior citizen, relative, or school employee whose interest in children isn't exhausted by their job. An attentive, outside-the-classroom listener is so encouraging that it pays rich dividends to make sure each student has someone.

Ask Designated Listeners to think through a plan and a time of day when they can do this, and commit to five to ten minutes in which the student explains to them everything new learned that day. The planned time, of course, may lead to talking about anything else. They might also ask questions from previous material, find out what the student considers important or interesting, and concentrate always on what he or she can already talk about successfully.

To help Designated Listeners, you can compile guidelines, suggest communication skills from the CSCS (Appendix 9), make up a check-off calendar they can post on their refrigerator, or send home the five factors for Perfect Conversation, the questions for exploring a topic (cf. 14) and the perspectives for understanding (cf. 26) for older students. Designated Listeners (especially parents) might wish to meet occasionally to discuss how to make their few minutes fruitful, support the class in other ways, and help each other solve the many practical problems they encounter in aiding their children's education.

Two qualities make this activity welcome to parents and different from other help they may provide. One is the limited but specific commitment of time, and the other is the focus on prior success. The hard work of installing the knowledge has already been done at school, and now comes the easy part that increases its value to students and integrates it into their thinking.

32. Primary Grades

Most of the methods of the Silver Bullet design adapt readily to primary grades. The steps aren't complicated, signals of effort are evident, rewards come quickly, emotional needs are met, and simple criteria assure them that they meet expectations.

For conveying knowledge to them, two compelling points of access are their imagination and their concreteness. Experiences, hands-on activity, stories, posters, and pictures impress images into their heads.

The output phase for them is to tell the story of their learning: Tell how they care for the guinea pig, tell about the seasons, tell how to make bread, tell about the calendar, tell the story of Arnold's adventure, tell about *The Little Engine That Could*, tell about any historical event or person, tell what they learned on the field trip; tell about colors, letters, words, and numbers; tell about the world! Their performance is to tell their story to a listening partner.

If the picture of one kindergartner listening attentively to another challenges credulity, note that it's a behavior comprised of a scant few concrete details easily conveyed: 1) Keep your mouth shut, 2) look at the other student, and 3) wait till they're done. We can drill such guidelines until they master them, and then insert quantities of knowledge into them. The means of doing this is to give them a simple instruction they repeat out loud and then perform together.

Stand them in two rows facing each other. In their own row, they're side by side with others and looking toward someone who stands in a similar row a couple of feet away. One row might place their toes on a strip of red paper. Say to them, "You're the Reds." The others toe a green strip: "You're the Greens." (Teach any two things this way with pictures on the floor: red whales and green elephants, crickets and beetles, ships and planes, and so on.) Ask them all to point to their partner opposite and make sure pairs find each other. Then practice the micro-steps one at a time:

"Reds, raise your hands." They do. They know who they are.

"Reds, I want you to ask a question of the Greens. Now what are you going to do?"

They answer in chorus, "Ask a question of the Greens!"

You say again, "Reds, I want you to ask a question of the Greens. Now what are you going to do?"

Again they answer and stragglers chime in, "Ask a question of the Greens."

"Greens, I want you to answer the question. Now, what will you do?"

They shout together, "Answer the question!"

Then, "Reds, after you ask the question of your partner, you'll listen to their answer. Now, what will you do after you ask the question?" They respond, "Listen to the answer!" Do the same thing with the Greens.

Get them to repeat the directions in increments as small as needed until everyone has them cold. Then feed them content one question at a time for which you've supplied the answer, starting with the familiar for guaranteed success:

"When I tell you the question, I want you to say it to your partner right after me. So Reds, the first question to ask your partner is, 'What is your name?'" They do so in a babble of voices. You ask them to switch roles with the same question.

Clear maps. To get to this point, you gave them a clear map of what to do. They repeated the map till all knew it, and then they carried it out with content added. With this basic sequence, address any points of learning you wish. Tell questioners what to ask and answerers what to answer. When everyone has mastered school rules and classroom guidelines, proceed into points of knowledge. At times they help each other make sure "all the steps are in the right order," or "all the parts are there." You may wish to score their collective ability to tell back their knowledge and compile the class's growing number of points of knowledge on a wall chart while assuring everyone of 100% success. All are encouraged to notice that they measure up to expectations perfectly.

Two goals are to install both knowledge and the pattern that does this. The latter is the more critical. They wonder, "What do I do first? What do I do next? And then?" They 1) line up, 2) identify a partner, 3) get the question straight, 4) identify the source of the answer such as on a wall chart or in a book or in your ringing words, 5) ask the question, 6) give the answer, and 7) trade roles. When they learn that answer, they 8) identify the next thing to learn.

Eight steps comprise a system they can use to learn anything, while its reciprocity and energy make it seem like a game they always win at. Drill the map of the action steps, run it for a few days, and they have it perfectly. The less clear it is, the more likely they'll back off. If they've learned to fear mistakes, they think, "I'm not going to try this seriously until I know I won't be embarrassed," and they wait till they're certain they can do it successfully. Once they can operate it on their own, it's your permanent, cost-free ally.

A way for primary students to master and claim their learning is:

1. On an index card, they write a question on the front and its answer on the back, and collect their cards in a personal box labeled **Memory Bank**.
2. They practice each card until they can tell it without looking at it that day, and consider it mastered when they can do this on three separate days, which they note on the card.
3. They make up a duplicate card to take home and present to their parents. Parents are encouraged to ask them the question, listen to the answer, celebrate their competence, and deposit the duplicates in a home Memory Bank on the kitchen table for ongoing use.

33. Memory Hooks

The most basic memory device is the intrinsic structure of a subject that illuminates how everything relates to everything else. Artificial aids can help but run the risk of removing the focus from the subject. Students may later remember the hooks perfectly without connecting them to the knowledge. Memory books offer many suggestions, but I'd like to pass along a couple I've found useful.

A **number code** links the sound of certain letters to specific numbers. With the code, you can compose a phrase easy to remember, the words of which give you a clue to the meaning and sequence of the numbers. A common code is 1= the letter T (think of the single downstroke of the letter); 2= the letter N (two downstrokes), 3 = M (three downstrokes), 4 = R (rr sound in four), 5 = L (Roman numeral for 50), 6 = CH, SH, J (the chuh, shuh, juh sound), 7 = hard K sound (both sounds in "cake"), 8 = F (think of the double loop of the cursive f), 9 = B, P (letters b and p are both inversions of 9), and 0 = S, Z, and soft C (as in "zero" and "city").

Using just the first consonant of a word to represent its number, you can translate number sequences into a clue about their meaning. The first five digits of *pi* might translate clumsily as "Move Turns Round To Join," the initial consonants indicating 3.1416. Columbus happening upon America in 1492 becomes "Traveling aRmada Pinta Nina," again using the first consonant encountered in each word. Class creativity can convert formulas, mathematical relationships, and dates into phrases all can learn.

A framework for remembering a sequence of ideas is to select a **visual analogy** for a given point of knowledge and join it to a naturally occurring sequence you can picture easily.

Once I gained almost total recall of a difficult course by placing it all on two streets I was familiar with near my home (the "loci" method). I'd identify a point I wanted to remember, invent a visual analogy for it, and locate it beside a house I knew well. I'd work my way around the house, placing the analogical forms near windows, corners, fences, and yard characteristics I could recall, and then move to the next house. To indicate an ascending sequence I used a ladder propped beside a door; for a reference to a part and whole, a large pie with pieces cut; a concept contained within another was a small can nested inside a larger one, and so on.

An unexpected benefit of the method was that the effort to represent an abstract concept visually pressed me to understand it, and I found myself readily integrating ideas later. A similar technique works well also for remembering the substance of a lecture. I'd pick a familiar room, assign visual symbols to the points of the lecture, and place them clockwise around the room, which helped me understand them, recall their substance, and have time pass quickly.

Represent knowledge. Individuals hold onto knowledge by different handles, mainly seeing (visual), hearing/saying (auditory), and feeling/doing (kinesthetic). Regardless of the aspects of intelligence in which students may be strong or weak, we need to enable everyone to bridge into a common fund of shared knowledge. To overlap, we 1) use multiple forms of representation in *presenting* knowledge, and 2) students bridge from one form to another in *expressing* it. Whatever the form of input the student prefers, the output phase can include the others. An all-purpose vehicle is *for teachers to describe in words the abstractions, pictures, diagrams and structural forms, and for students to write, explain, and perform them.* A student who relies mainly on hearing words picks up sounds and then puts visuals to them. One who appreciates the pictures and diagrams listens also for the words and then speaks them. One who best writes them, listens, watches, and speaks. They receive knowledge as they best do so, translate it inwardly to the other forms needed, and output the expanded knowledge.

Students who appear to gather much from presentation and discussion and little from reading may be predominantly auditory. I once knew a doctor who'd graduated from medical school without taking notes, to the consternation of his teachers. He sat in the front row and just remembered everything spoken. If you guess such a bent, you might ask

"Would you rather 'Play the tape' or 'See the movie' for remembering what we've discussed?"

"Does this come through your mind word by word?"

"Do you often recall what people say verbatim?"

"Do you get more from my explanations or from reading by yourself?"

If they're auditory, suggest that they "replay what I just said" instead of picturing it.

Pictures. Many textbooks have a wonderful array of illustrations. Ask them to scan the pictures in their text and employ a visual memory method such as Mental Movie.

Diagrams. Kevin, one of my students who was intelligent and artistic, complained that he couldn't remember things the way others did. Knowing his ability, I asked him to convert each key idea into a visual symbol and link up the day's assignment in a creative way. He was able to do this almost as fast as he could write, and had the material learned in few minutes. Use students' special abilities.

Structuring. Many students benefit from parts fitting together into logical structures. One way to master a subject is to spend the first few days learning the table of contents of the text. Talk through it to help them understand how chapters fit the whole, and use the Time Capsule method or Content Scoreboard chunk by chunk to retain it perfectly (cf. 36 and 47). Then as you proceed through the text in more detail, every new idea finds a logical place in a structure ever more deeply understood and reinforced.

Make it a class project to develop interesting ways to assimilate knowledge. They might invent diagrams, an association of images, time lines, causal relationships, visual or logical structures, and imaginative links. Ask them to outline what they want to remember and then devise the easiest way for everyone to grasp it.

Kinesthetics. Those who represent knowledge through physical sensations benefit especially from writing out lecture notes and summaries. Invite them to draw outlines, maps, and symbolic representations. Physical movement can also aid their effort to represent qualities difficult for them to put into words. The Total Physical Response method succeeds in teaching foreign languages by drawing on how intimately we enlist our physical system in our way of perceiving and manifesting meaning in language (cf. tprsource.com).

Writing. Ask them to create a synthesis of the notes they accumulate from your presentations and their own reading. They write out a summary and place it with the answers in their notebooks. Re-organizing and summarizing is one of the fastest ways to gain in-depth understanding and insures that the material can safely be laid aside for a longer time and with brief review still be grasped completely.

34. Concentration Units

The value of any class activity increases as students concentrate on it. They 1) choose a focus or goal, 2) identify the activity that reaches the goal, 3) maintain their attention to it, and 4) ignore distractions.

Offer Albert Einstein as a model. From many years of self-discipline, he reported that he'd trained himself to concentrate without letup for as long as forty-five minutes. When he was deep in his work and a distractive thought came up, he would say to himself, "I will not permit that to distract me again," and make a tally on a pad nearby. Doing so was a motivation because it annoyed him.

Measuring something accurately makes it easier to manage. Two scores form a concentration unit. One is their level of concentration as a percentage. Einstein's near-perfect focus is at the top, overcoming instantly any threat diverting them from their work. The bottom is their vulnerability to the slightest influence. At 10%, a student is barely paying attention, at 30% perhaps trying to study with a boy or girl friend sitting nearby, and at 60% substantially following a teacher's presentation with the mind wandering periodically.

The other measure is the amount of time they spend at that level. Combining the ratings, we obtain a CU by multiplying the percent of concentration times the number of minutes it persists, so that 50% concentration for a 50 minute period = 2,500 CUs.

Their greatest gain comes not from a small change in their number of minutes in class but from a large change in their concentration. A distracted class operating at a 10% concentration for **50 minutes** achieves 10 x 50 or 500 CUs per student. A more focused class with a 50% concentration level for **45 minutes** achieves 45 x 50 or 2250 CUs, and raising their concentration to 80% even while reducing its time to **40 minutes** still increases their CUs to 3200. Such changes in score are a clue to why effective class work can dramatically increase their learning. Alertness to their personal level stimulates self-management: "Hmm. I'm letting myself be distracted. Gotta focus."

Invite them to estimate their concentration for the current hour and turn in their results to you. Post their scores until the next time you ask the same question and then insert the new numbers. In asking students to rate themselves, I've found that they usually do so close to the score I'd assign from watching them. For variety, have them draw another student's name randomly, and without saying whom they're observing, rate themselves and the other at the end of the class. They turn in both and you average them all for a class score you post on a line chart.

Resolving subtle issues can increase concentration. A high school math teacher told me that she spent the first ten minutes of every class talking with students about their feelings, and always got more done with the remaining time than when she tried to spend the entire period on math. Surging feelings can seize attention as much as does a bulldozer working outside the window.

35. Walk Away

For years I was curious about how to deepen my own learning. One day I ran across a study in a journal printed probably in the fifties or sixties (that's eluded my attempts to track it down) reporting on the authors' attempt to determine the most effective use of time in education. How long should students spend at what activity in order to enhance long term retention of knowledge? The choices were the usual classroom activities of reading, writing, lecturing, note-taking, and styles of study. The answer they found could revolutionize educational outcomes. The most efficient time use was spending 40% to 80% of it in **the effort to recall.** We apply such effort when we explain an idea to someone else or take a test. Test-taking, it's been found, enhances memory even of material not tested (19).

The steps of the Walk Away method adapt this idea. 1) We install a piece in our memory, 2) recall it at intervals, 3) increase the size of the pieces, and 4) increase the length of the interval between rehearsals of it. I would use these steps for twenty minutes daily to master course notes, spend a concentrated weekend absorbing a semester's notes, or practice giving a talk.

First, select the material you want to learn, such as passages in your textbook or notes, and open them on a table. Instead of sitting as you usually do to study, stand up in front of the material. The activity requires more disciplined attention, so you want to convey to your mind that it must produce differently than usually happens when you sit. The standing position also enables you to move about.

You might lean over the material and look down, with your hands planted on the table on either side of it. Being slightly uncomfortable reminds you not to relax there because you'll move on in a moment. Read for two to four minutes, more briefly if the material is dense and fact-filled, and longer if it's more general. Try to fix in your mind the concepts you want to save and the key words and phrases that synthesize them. Limit yourself to three to five points at a time, working within the precision level and chunk size that fit your study goals (cf. 38. Degrees of Precision). After you select the points, scan them for twenty to thirty seconds and fix them in your mind. Put words to this process: "Okay, there's this, point one (summarize it), and now . . . ah, here's point two (say inwardly the words that describe it). I'll include also this, point three (say it) and here's point four (say it). That's enough." Putting words to the focus of your attention makes it more definite (20).

Straighten up, walk to the other side of the room, **and aloud tell back all you can remember of what you read**. This reveals exactly what you know.

In doing this, you alter your intent. While I read, it seldom occurs to me to say, "Do I know this or not?" Ideas flow along like a highway under my automobile. I point myself toward where I'm going rather than to where I've been. This method instead causes me to look backward. Saying the words aloud makes clear just how much of where I've been still lodges in me.

When you've exhausted your memory and paused long enough to extract final bits, walk back to the material on the table. Look at it again and identify the portions remembered and those not. If you recalled points two and four and missed one and three, fix the missing pieces where they belong and repeat—walking away and recalling everything with all the pieces included. Continue these steps—re-reading, re-fixing the material in your mind, and then walking away to recount them—until you have that chunk learned completely. Go to another chunk, do the same with it, and combine the two, telling back everything in them.

Its unique features enhance the method. **Standing** during it signals an active experience replacing physical positions unconsciously associated with leisure. **Walking away** signals the memory that you won't rescue it from the effort to recall, and prevents you from gathering hints by quick glances at the material. You tell your mind to **produce everything,** which is the criterion memory activity. **Saying the words aloud** (or whispered if others are nearby) clarifies exactly what you know and don't know. Studying wordlessly may leave you believing that you know what really remains unspecified.

36. Time Capsule

The title of the method refers to *capsules* of selected knowledge carried forward in *time*. The method is easy to use, generates vivid and permanent memory, and is especially useful in subjects requiring precise recall such as foreign languages, mathematics, and science (cf. 38. Degrees of Precision).

In developing it, I wanted a way to refine the effort to recall (cf. 35). I asked my fifteen-year-old son if he would try out my design.

"Six minutes a day max, total time spent," I said.

"No problem," he reported. "So what do you want me to learn?" The end of school was three weeks off. I was curious what he would choose, so I was generously vague.

"Pick anything you like, anything you'd want to talk to someone about, anything you'd want to have as permanent learning." He drew material for five days learning from articles about rock groups and drum technique.

We applied the method described below (without boxing the capsules). He recalled the information at the intervals specified, with the total time spent in all of the recalls together around six minutes a day. As expected, he remembered perfectly everything he installed in the two minutes of study we allotted daily for his initial reading. At the end of the week I asked him casually, "Do you think you might want to use this method with some of your subjects?"

"Yeah," he answered. "Maybe when we start studying for finals." In eleven days his school would be out. Before that, his teachers would pass a few pieces of the semester's work through students' minds one last time and then test the pieces. I sighed.

Years later when I mentioned to him that I was writing about his experience, he said, "Funny thing is, Dad, I still remember that stuff!" If his teachers had wanted to install anything from their courses permanently, they could have asked students **to obtain a clear initial impression of the knowledge and then expand the interval between recalls of it.** If other methods of impressing knowledge are used (such as Total Physical Response or foreign language immersion), the Time Capsule method efficiently consolidates the learning. It picks up when the material is already learned to the point that a test on it would result in a standard bell curve of results. The remaining step is to insure that everyone retains it permanently (a hockey-stick curve—everyone clustered at the upper end).

Forming capsules. To form a capsule, express the learning in concise phrases, write them in a compact form, and draw a border around them.

Maybe in preparing for a difficult exam in college, you distilled a course into two pages of key notes. It's the same idea, except that you apply that level of attention throughout the semester. Though you may explain much about a given issue, you specify the points that deserve perfect recall as you proceed, the key material you'd want on a comprehensive test. The boundary around a piece of learning identifies *what deserves extra effort.* A high school science teacher decided that the eight signs of cancer should be permanent learning for her students, made a capsule of them, and everyone learned them as I watched. Material goes into a capsule because you want to focus on it in exactly that form.

You might designate a subject and let students choose details: "Read pages 85 to 90 in your social studies book and form capsules for ideas you pick out" or "Work on all the Spanish vocabulary you can for the remainder of the hour." Pages just for capsules can be added to the Answers section of their notebooks as a succinct expression of what they know, with matching questions on their Questions pages.

Capsule size. Capsules are brief, of a size students can grasp and assimilate readily, but too little in them means insufficient challenge while too much overtaxes the memory. The denser the material is, the smaller the capsule needs to be and the shorter its initial reading time; such as mastering *pi* to seven digits or a single math formula. You know the meaning of numbers, symbols, and words already and the links between them are evident (e.g. to multiply or divide). To find the right size, **read a capsule slowly and thoughtfully once. If you can look up, be slightly challenged by it but repeat it accurately,** then it's probably ideal. If you can't repeat it, read it one more time. If you still can't repeat it, it's too big. Cut it by a fifth or a quarter.

Weigh the information contained in both **points and bits,** which challenge the mind differently. *Points* are the part you don't know, the piece of knowledge you want to add. Four or five of these in one capsule work well. Points are expressed by words, symbols, or numbers you already know, which I refer to as *bits,* each adding an essential note of meaning. Because they may be few or many, they present a somewhat separate challenge. One new point explained by a paragraph of familiar bits (words) may become unwieldy.

Selecting the bits that express a point efficiently is a valuable cognitive task. Missing a few might leave vagueness acceptable in some subjects but not in others. Best results seem to occur with capsules of between ten and twenty bits of total information (words and numbers) but no more than seven new points. You might have five Spanish words and their English translations or arrange the new words in one to three phrases or sentences. For instance:

Q. Give four forms of the Spanish verb "to talk."

Q. What was the great mission to find India that failed?

hablar—to talk
hablo—I talk
hablas—you (familiar) talk
habla—he/she talks

The first capsule contains fourteen bits, four of them novel (the Spanish vocabulary to learn) and the other ten arranged in four phrases possessing familiar order. The second contains twenty bits arranged in seven points—three names of people, three boats, and a date.

Preparing capsules. Prepare capsules the day before installing them if possible. When everyone understands their format and size, you can ask them to create one for the class from a page you assign them individually. When all are ready, they present their capsule to the group, discuss each one, improve it as needed, and copy them all into their notebooks.

In preparing capsules while they install others, students shouldn't see reminders of the prior material. They leave from and return cleanly to what

King Ferdinand and Queen Isabella of Portugal sent Christopher Columbus with three ships, the Pinta, Nina, and Santa Maria in 1492.

they're installing, covering up capsules already in process or studying a different subject. Master science, for example, while reading history between recalls. Master math capsules while working on easy material in language arts. If you have them just for one subject, at least direct them to non-overlapping work.

This is a good day-end activity for small groups, can occupy scattered pockets of time, and makes the next day more productive. The mind does much of its work spontaneously during sleep if it's fed information and given an expectation (21). Being told, "Tomorrow you're going to master this perfectly," their minds attack it automatically. The next day before opening their notebooks they ask themselves, "What are we installing today?" Recalling the basic subject matter and an impression of the prepared capsules, half their work is done, assuring them rapid success. The material, again, is already presented, understood, prioritized, boundaried, and arranged. All that remains is permanent retention.

Steps to install. Try this out yourself. Read over a capsule you've prepared and understand the information in it. Then get a first impression you'll call up repeatedly with a 100% accurate, complete, internal representation with all points and bits in place, general ideas and details:

Read it, lay it down, look away, visualize it and immediately repeat in words everything you can remember. Saying everything in words, telling all the bits at least whispered to yourself is the only way to determine for sure what you know. If you can't put words to it immediately, you don't have exact knowledge. Describe visual elements. In a formula, put all the symbols, numbers, and steps in their right places. For lists, describe the placement of ideas—first, second, and third.

Once you can do this—read, look up, and tell the whole thing—you have an initial fix on it. Compare it to hammering a nail. The first tap gets it in the right position but secured only superficially. The next taps drive it in solidly but depend absolutely on the first one done well. As yet, the material is only lightly embedded in memory.

Set a timer for one minute later. A minute is long enough to give your memory a challenge. For sixty seconds, turn your attention to something else, specifically not thinking about your first impression. Unless you focus elsewhere, you don't tax your memory to hold onto it. If the capsule remains visible on your desk or included in something else you look at, your mind doesn't mount an effort to remember. Use a clock with a sweep second hand if you don't have a timer that beeps, but appoint someone to call time at the end of each interval or do it yourself.

When the timer goes off, do the recall. After the minute, *don't look at the material*. Recall everything you can from it. Only after you've tried your best and can't remember it all, go back and study briefly any part you forgot. Look at the capsule, *again recall it instantly* and repeat the one-minute interval until you can tell it back perfectly without hesitating or re-checking. Complete recall usually occurs on the first try because you already know the material well and the interval is short. From there, the avenue to permanent memory is clear: *just increase the interval.*

Set the timer for five minutes later. Engage your attention in something else. When the timer rings after five minutes, repeat what you did after one minute. Recall the capsule as completely as you can before checking or reviewing it in print. Don't go back to the printed version at all unless details have dropped from memory. Repeat absolutely everything in words and include any details you missed before. If you can't, reread it to fill in the missing pieces and repeat the same step or return to the prior interval of one minute. Some students prefer a three minute interval. Those of three to five minutes seem comparable for continuing the cycle.

Expand intervals. The next intervals are fifteen minutes, forty-five to sixty minutes, several hours or day's end, and preferably for the two days following. Then include it in students' long-range mastery review to be recalled occasionally. When students are successful at the fifteen minute time, they have an impression deep enough to be easily refreshed and practiced later.

Group collaboration. Students enjoy the challenge of installing several capsules in one period. Three are easy. A different student times each one, starts off its intervals, and calls time when they're completed. Everyone begins their recall together for each capsule at the immediate and one minute phases till all are successful. Then while the first is in its five minute interval, a second is introduced that doesn't have overlapping content. With two in progress (one to its five and the other to its fifteen minute interval), a third can be initiated. Between recalls, the group can prepare capsules on new material and share and copy them.

When two capsules complete an interval at about the same time, they're always of different length. Each timer tells the interval for their capsule, and everyone recalls the shortest first since it's the most tenuous. The longer the interval, the deeper the capsule is already embedded and better able to sustain a delay. So if capsules with five, fifteen, and forty-five minute intervals come up together, recall the five first, then the fifteen, and then the forty-five minute. Write on the board the list of intervals:

immediate
1 minute
3-5 minutes
12-15 minutes
45-60 minutes
3 hours or end of day

A kitchen timer with a quiet beep is handy for setting intervals. I've used three at a time with one set at a minute, one at five, and one at fifteen minutes. Cognitive styles may relate to the task slightly differently. Auditory students emphasize talking out a capsule as though hearing it on headphones a word at a time and kinesthetics may add analogical body movement or imagine doing so.

CHAPTER 6

Focus Learning

W e make many decisions about where to focus both the manner and content of students' thinking. A few considerations can aid our choices.

37. Use Maps

Imagine a family planning a vacation to the Grand Canyon. Later, smart kid number two sees his father looking at a map of New England and says, "Dad, why are you looking at New England if we're going to the Grand Canyon?" He presumes that a direction of focus is a direction for action.

We can think of maps as a set of directions that channel behavior, a sequence of internal representations for upcoming actions. Learning a map adjusts the system to proceed accordingly. When their maps generate problems, we need one ourselves to return them to collaboration with school practices. We first install the thinking that makes desired action at least possible (they know what to do) and then that makes it easy and pleasant (assured success with a positive emotional tone).

The power of a mental map to organize learning came home to me one day at a coffee shop. I happened to converse with Dan, who'd had some difficulties in his life, turned a corner, and at the time had a job in which he was doing well. He'd spent several months at an employment center to raise his skills, and told me about the first math class.

This big group was sitting there. None of us had done well in school. The teacher comes in and the first thing he says is, "Okay, who can tell me how to calculate the square root of 49?" He stared at us, looking from one to another. We all lowered our heads and thought, "Uh-oh. This is going to be bad." After a long silence, he says, "Alright, I'll tell you. The answer is A, B, C." He wrote on the board A, B, C and said, "It's only one step and another step and another step. And this is what you need to remember. Every single problem you meet is exactly the same, just A, B, C." And that's the way he taught us so that everybody

learned. Every problem just boiled down to A, B, C. All math was just a series of steps, and we learned the steps.

A wise teacher conveyed a general map for reading the other maps students would encounter, and they gained confidence that they could learn a subject that till then had befuddled them. Like the math teacher above, transmit the map before you ask for the behavior. If the steps are A and B and C, develop ABC in their minds as a mental unit. Without this, action is hesitant and far harder to coordinate. The more people affected by an activity, the clearer the map must be for everyone. Without maps for new behaviors, students (like teachers) tend to act randomly or return to old behaviors.

Become aware of your own. We devise inwardly what we want to accomplish. You might lay out a versatile pathway to a daily objective: **students exerting constant effort that always seems stimulating to them**. Imagine you're a coach. Everything else depends on how you manage effort and attitude. Winning a game that's days or weeks in the future is outside your power. Available today are effort and attitude that maximize the benefit from every minute spent. Examine carefully how your map supports or detracts from that objective.

Use awareness and flexibility with your map. With your purpose clearly in mind, you need two other tools. One is the ability to observe sensitively whether or not you're getting what you want. Your *awareness* informs you of what's happening in front of you, ascertains your current results. If you misread the situation, your strategy is sure to misfire. Your other tool is your set of *flexible responses* for how to manage what you encounter (22). These include all the methods you've learned as a teacher.

Put words to what you notice in order to activate the link between your awareness and your possible responses. Perhaps today you want them to talk to each other better. Seeing them in animated involvement, you voice these thoughts to yourself:

Ah, I see some skills used. Good! There's attention to each other, and a brief silence over there. He's thinking about what someone said. And these three are commenting on the same topic! They've had four sentences now on the same issue with no one veering off. Good going. I can let them proceed a few minutes more. I'll talk to Jeremy later about interrupting.

In your map, you 1) notice their behavior carefully, 2) describe the advances in skill you observe, 3) offer accurate feedback, 4) shape by giving guidelines, and 5) welcome their perceptions of their progress.

Create an expectation. Post something, announce something, make a prediction, begin preparations, or confer about arrangements: "Can you move your desks? Turn and face this way. We're doing something new today." Pointing them toward pending action awakens an *action set,* stimulating neurologically the array of capacities they'll use.

Teach the map before asking for the behavior. Their cooperation in learning the map forecasts that they'll follow it. Focusing on a map, their unconscious gets an implied command, "You're going to do this, so get ready." Later you call on the map and discover your prophetic accuracy. There they are, doing what they had in mind to do. Project ahead: "We're going to start this on Wednesday." Outline the steps they'll use and have them learn them to put group consensus to work. They notice that everyone is learning the steps. As you fill their minds with details, everyone appears to agree, implying that they will too.

Make the map clear. They must have the activity clear. A kindergarten teacher gets 100% cooperation teaching a four-step map: "Everyone gets a piece of cake if you do four things: One, take a napkin. Two, put a piece of cake on it. Three, return to your seat. Four, eat the cake at your seat. I want everyone to learn the four steps before anyone takes a piece of cake." Try to make your maps just as clear. You might want to draw boxes on the board showing their steps: 1, 2, 3.

Demonstrate the map. Sometimes it's easier to show that to explain. Get several students in front of everyone, give them directions, walk them through the map, correct them if necessary, ask others what they observed, and then explain what else they should notice. A two-minute demonstration may be more efficient than re-explaining the map.

Free them to follow the map. To conduct the action by the map requires turning over control of it to students so they can follow the map instead of your commands. Watch what happens and confer later: How did it go? What went right? What diverged from the guideline? What should we change? Clarify the map and run the action again: "If the cake falls on the floor, go to the closet, get the dustpan and broom . . . ."

Regard failure to follow the map as a learning issue. If some students don't comply, proceed as if they'll come around. All you're asking at first is that they learn the steps of the map. Many are willing to watch something they feel awkward doing, yet this is still aligned to your purpose. Saying "You can sit and watch the group till you understand" presumes that they hesitate from lack of understanding or ease rather than from any negative quality in them. They're not yet able to mesh the activity with something about themselves—their place in the group, their self-image, or their fears of failure. Another detour that returns them to cooperation is to ask them to collect information about an activity with an observer's checklist, and report to you what they see.

Resolve structure. You might wonder how to tell when you need to create a new map. A clue is that it takes you several requests to get their attention. You don't want their signal to resume attention to you to be your exasperated plea, "Could we *please* get it quiet in here?" Your students at first may require tight control to manage them, may cooperate only gradually upon being coaxed and corrected, may be suspicious of new activities, wish not to be bothered, and the idea of discipline *during* an activity may be alien to them.

Our aim, again, is to channel energy clearly so that everyone agrees on what they're doing. We achieve this by managing key details precisely, reminiscent of my experience with cadets marching and of drill teams and football and soccer. While the following suggestions may seem at first to control details excessively, another way to think of them is by how you teach a child to wash dishes. To get the results you want, there's no escape from actually pointing out the details you want him/her to bring under control until a pattern incorporates that level of attention automatically. If students waste the class's time, you can't avoid attending to the details that redirect their behavior.

You might start by collecting evidence that there's a need, that this is not just you being cranky. You point out the problem of repeated delays. Many are bored waiting for others to cooperate, and you want to get on with the lesson. Count occurrences of delay for a baseline so you'll know you're making progress when they change.

One way is to use a digital timer to add up the cumulative time between when you call for their attention and when you have it, or when you ask them to begin an activity and they actually do so. Quantify to the second the time they waste in changing from one learning activity to another, and tell them at the end of the day how much was lost in all the transitions. You might draw two boxes side-by-side on the board, label them 1 and 2 with an arrow between them, and say:

> **I'd like to let you work together more. I think you might enjoy it, but there's a problem with that. It requires changing from one activity (#1 on the board) to another (#2) without wasting time. You'll get up, move to a partner, and begin talking with each other. In doing that, it's easy to get off the subject. So if you're going to work together, you need to be able to shift directly from learning individually to learning with partners. We need to see how quickly you can make that change, and then change back when the activity ends—two (#2) back to one (#1). First I'll explain what to do. Then I'll raise the timer and say "Go!" I'll start the timer, and you begin to carry out the plan. We'll keep track of the time you require in order to change from one thing to another, and then try to improve on it.**

You give them a clear map of what to do and the signals that start and end it, and then time the portion you want to improve. They rise, go to their partner, sit together, and ask and answer the questions. Time them from when you say "Begin" to when you see everyone engaged. Toward the end of the time, say, "Class, would you please end in a half-minute?" In thirty seconds, say "Please return to your seats" and time them from when you make the request to when it's fulfilled.

If transition time remains a problem, practice it several times in a row; three rounds doing the steps with different partners. Time them each round so they can monitor their progress (cf. Chapter 9 for one example of this approach).

Make a map for your own versatile response. If their group work deteriorates, your map about yourself guides. You might read their dysfunction as a message about their needs rather than about any negative qualities: "They really need clear ideas to go by, don't they!" Notice yourself interpret the situation in a way that restores you to selecting an effective response.

If you can't generate a proactive direction, you can retreat temporarily. If you've just tried discussion groups, 1) say "Well, let's end for today. Everyone seems a little distracted." 2) The next day, come back just to teaching the map: "Let's make sure everyone understands this and has it in mind. Remember the guidelines. Go over them with your partner and clarify any you don't understand." 3) Return to the activity as you see cooperation in learning the map: "Congratulations! Everyone learned those steps faster than I expected. So we have some time now to do the activity today. Here are your groups . . . ." As they use time well, 4) add more: "Everyone did so well yesterday that I'm going to add an extra five minutes. If your group ends early, take out some personal reading." 5) You might offer an appropriate incentive like self-managed time they can save up, or a reward they'd like to work toward (cf. Bonus Time in 28. Use Consequences).

One day's solution is less important than your strategy for reaching all kinds of solutions, how you'll respond to non-cooperation. Your map includes 1) recognizing need instead of opposition, 2) reality-checking by gathering information, 3) shifting to a positive attitude, 4) examining alternatives to find the most constructive, and 5) taking specific action. Like a play in sports, students need a plan, a signal that says "Go!" and action operating the plan: one, two, three. They like themselves better when their energy is focused and flows smoothly, and they like to follow coaches who know what they're doing. They're like soldiers: *Who will prepare himself for battle if the trumpet sounds an uncertain note?*

38. Degrees of Precision

Distinguish three levels of exactness and use the appropriate one for the task at hand.

Exact basics. For beginners, these are the names of things and facts about the world. Later, we learn countless ideas exactly: observations of the physical world, scientific and mathematical formulas and measurement systems, basic vocabulary and grammar, and terms for any discipline. Here also are structural elements, ways that subjects divide into part and whole, and fundamental principles discovered by centuries of investigation. Both their *selection* and *form* are already settled and must be assimilated as they are, so this learning offers a precise conclusion. We can know it completely at the level that concerns us now, and mastery of it enlarges our creative ability. The formula for the area of a circle and that "hablar" means "to talk" in Spanish apply to all circles and all instances of speaking in Spanish. Where learning is clearly identified and unanimously regarded as necessary, mastering it exactly is the basis for all later knowledge.

Elaborated applications. This adds specifics to everything found in the prior level: examples of formulas, uses of words, instances of generalization, details supporting basic ideas, the reasons and evidence and principles generating an insight. In this area, the *form* depends on something more exact that's learned already, but the *selection* of details can vary widely. Elementary students studying the formula for the area of a rectangle, for instance, have unlimited variables for different size objects. A foreign language vocabulary yields an endless variety of ideas drawing on the same word meanings.

Completeness for this zone is defined arbitrarily. Students might do 150 long division problems at varying degrees of difficulty before it's complete. The mastery of a given foreign language vocabulary word might be achieved with fluid use in five different contexts.

Narrative extension. This knowledge incorporates the entire world of experience. Where a given issue can be viewed from several angles, both the selection and form of what to learn vary with the current purpose. Think of history, geography, psychology, interpersonal dynamics, entertainment, literature, art, anthropology, personalized learning, and creativity. Beyond their exact basics, one can be right in many ways. With many perspectives feasible, the zone has no natural boundaries. Because every piece of knowledge can be connected potentially to others, teachers reasonably can allow students to set their own priorities and help them obtain as much knowledge in this zone as time allows. There's no reason for everyone to learn the same thing if they simply learn and can demonstrate something.

Understanding the difference between these levels helps guide students' practice. It's a tedious mistake to expect the same exactness in level two and three material that level one requires. And it's as egregious an error to leave the variance in level one material that's easily accommodated in level three. Knowledge at levels two and three can be shifted and changed. Freezing it tends to march the mind in set tracks. Flexibility with level one material, however, courts disaster. Rocket seals need to fit, parts need to articulate, train crossing lights need to work, the surgeon's knife must cut exactly, and both speaker and listener should derive the same meaning from a word.

One of my students illustrated the three levels of precision, a dyslexic eighth grade boy reading at the third grade level. For years he'd endured labels, special classes, and fruitless attempts to help him while his anger and discouragement grew. Trying him at various reading tasks and watching him closely for a few days, I discovered that no one had ever taught him the vowel sounds needed to decipher words. During eight years in the public school system, no one had addressed this basic need. In a couple weeks of practicing these exactly (level one) and applying them to simple words under my oversight (level two), he took off. Year-end tests rated him as covering five years of reading (level three) in a year. A similar instance was an intelligent fifth grade boy struggling with some aspects of first grade math. Taking him through the micro-steps of simple problems and inquiring about his thought processes, I discovered that for years he'd been confused about the difference between multiply and divide. Exact basics have to be taught exactly.

39. Save Basics

From the body of information presented, extract the synthesis, key fact, or element of structure you want them to save. What's the core jewel you want them to carry forward that's worth the extra effort? Each of the following can be converted to a Learning Feat with Q and A, and scored.

If you use **new terms** they don't understand to explain concepts they don't understand, they're likely to learn both by rote. Compile terms into a meaningful set. An upper elementary math glossary may contain 200, mastery of which could be spread through a year. Include the rules associated with each one's use, its order in any sequence or formula, and problems that employ it. You can use the Content Scoreboard (cf. 47) for learning twenty terms at a time.

The **structure** of a subject is probably the easiest way to understand everything else about it. Diagram it, and check whether your text's table of contents is the best arrangement. When you can, leave it to them to select what else to master. Beyond the terms and structure essential for their grade level, a range of knowledge might be valid learning. Check whether they understand it, put it into a form to master, and master it. Once they understand how to apply their effort, you can transfer more management of it to them. For everyone to work on something different they need only arrange it by Q and A, practice it, and score it.

Experiences, physical activity or hands-on aspects link their sensory system to the less tangible, making associated ideas easier to absorb: handling measuring devices, assembling pieces, bodily movement, or use of tools. Narrating the behavioral steps of gathering information can make it easier to retain. Field notes can be re-written, shared, and explained back and forth. Work products, experiments, exploration, and lab work can be documented with a personal logbook showing date, place, activity, results, and time spent and then organized as Q and A.

Easy details. Pausing briefly to recall who said what in a discussion can help them capture alternate perspectives. Reviewing how individuals responded to a topic fills in an overall summary (cf. 8. Go For It in 21). Episodes, events, physical activity, sequences, raw data, and imaginative images stick readily in the mind. Reorganize them as you add more refined knowledge. To insure a successful start of the school year that includes those who have difficulties in reading or writing, use material easy for everyone to draw from: multi-sensory presentations, video or CD-based lessons, or programs by Nature, Nova, or National Geographic. Often service activities contain a learning residue. Ask students to identify a question that elicits it and the points or steps that summarize it. My students and I repaired a table in six steps that became part of their learning.

After they've gathered what you want them to learn, employ some form of the effort to recall, such as with the Impromptu Performance, Mental Movie, Partner Practice, Peg List, Walk Away, and Time Capsule methods.

Since you want assimilated knowledge from them, use **audio-visual sources** slightly differently. Assimilating means taking a bite, chewing it, and swallowing it before taking another bite—permanence with something rather than coverage of everything. Working with CDs, DVDs, videos, or audio tapes, avoid the temptation to finish them prematurely. They typically present too much to absorb in one sitting. Install the important parts of just a segment. The rest will spend the night safely in its jacket, ready to be more stimulating the next day because they know something about it today:

Take notes and identify questions while students watch or listen.

Halt the tape every ten to fifteen minutes.

Pose a question from that section, pause for everyone to recall, and draw a name randomly to answer.

Do this with all the points from that portion.

They close their eyes and run it in their mind.

As time allows, they record the questions and answers in their notebooks that summarize it.

They tell it to a partner.

40. Learn Everything

Students are surrounded by boundaries of ignorance in every direction. A world of knowledge awaits and, I believe, *all should be welcome at school, not just course requirements*. Reasonably, we want each to learn as much as possible and graduate a polymath.

Start with a large question and fill it in gradually. You might organize thirteen years by dividing the universe of knowledge into, say, fifty subjects like science, mathematics, language, literature, foreign language, politics, economics, religion, philosophy, environment, anthropology, psychology, geology, ecology, community, sports, business, biography, health, family, learning methods, personal development, fiction, the arts (culture, music, art, theater), history (world, American, regional), and the world today. Include subjects of local interest like ethnic studies, the history and literature of different cultures, flora and fauna, coastlines, mountains, desert, industry, agriculture, resource extraction, and occupations unique to the area. Expect them every year to save what they learned before, add to every category, and **tell about the entire field with a comprehensive and detailed explanation:** "Tell all you know about geography," "Tell all you know about government," and "Tell all you know about health." They begin their answer with the structure of the subject, divide it into chunks and sub-chunks, and explain each separately.

They tell it to each other. When teachers must ask all the questions themselves, the time they can spend with each student is limited, making long answers prohibitive. Hearing out a single student could monopolize an entire period while most are coasting. The problem is similar to having a Grand Coulee Dam and just one pipe for the water to pass through. The solution is more pipes. We enlist half the class to listen to the other half.

As a set, the **varied questions** about it make knowledge more flexible. If you've just written a paragraph on the board, you can ask, "What question is this the answer to?" They suggest alternatives and personally pick one to elicit that answer. As they mature, it becomes more important that they begin learning the questions to which life itself will provide the answers.

Encourage each to become the **class expert** about a subject. Help them pick one and in performances ask them what they've learned about it.

Integrate piecemeal information into larger questions. Often pieces come from fill-in blanks, questions and answers at the ends of chapters, and definitions. In subjects requiring exact mastery of bits such as sciences, you may wish at first to teach single points answering single questions. A rapid stream of them can involve everyone with doses of success, and demonstrate to students with low confidence that they can learn. We don't want to sacrifice understanding, however. Explaining proceeds up a continuum of complexity as students integrate bits into longer answers. Questions about rules for capitalizations, commas, and sentence structure can be combined into one: "As though you were teaching the class, tell what you know about rules of grammar, give examples of each, and when and why you'd use them." The effort nudges students toward developing a mental checklist they can apply later, and to sort individual ideas by where they belong in a synthesis.

You might think at first, "I don't have time for that." If you don't, it's because you use the time for something else. If you provide them the basic information efficiently, they have time for developing mental skills they otherwise wouldn't draw on.

Answer expansion. They stay invested in old knowledge better by combining it with new. The two together make revising more effective. Changes occur in the region of the mid-brain used for motivation and reward-processing (23). Assign them an individual search: "When we review your question, we'll ask you what you've found for us." They can return to written sources and look for new details others can add to their notes and explanations. Enlarging and restructuring answers stimulate flexibility and assimilation (24). As students add new material, they can insert sheets in their notebooks at the appropriate places. For scoring it, if it doesn't alter the form of what they already know well, they can increase their score on that question without re-telling previous material.

41. Divide Subjects

When most students are competent in gathering and organizing knowledge, you can let them divide and share it. Each learns a piece and teaches it to others. Depending on the scope of the assignment, this may occur in a single period, a day, or in longer-term work. It can be done in pairs, organization groups, or other teams you configure.

In a small group, one at a time they lay on the table in front of others the questions and answers they've written out, and explain them. Others clarify, offer their own experiences and insights, add ideas from other sources, summarize the contributions, and copy them into their notebooks. The group then might use pairs to practice explaining what they've collected, or defer practice to another day.

Use a multi-text approach in either of two ways. You can stop at the point that each one gathers information for themselves or can arrange for them to exchange it.

In the first case 1) assign each student a specific source or let them select it. 2) They develop notes on their Answers pages with matching questions on their Questions pages, and 3) with a partner, practice the answer along with their other learning, and then 4) score it.

In the second case they 1) identify the information they want to share, 2) write a Q and A summary clearly enough that others can copy it, 3) share what they learned in pairs or groups, 4) copy each other's summaries, 5) practice the new learning with a partner, and 6) score it.

42. Focus on progress

Everyone would like to focus on progress instead of deficit, but "catching them doing it right" is easy to violate. We feel obligated to point out errors, and the number of errors then becomes our negative measure of the student (25). The Silver Bullet design instead is a way to mark progress entirely through successes.

One teacher noted rapid benefit from crediting her special needs students with all the new, correct answers they could add to prior assignments. They were incredulous at first because raising their scores felt to them like cheating, but her value was on more correct answers. She let them add as much new material as they were willing to undertake. When they realized that she wasn't mistake-oriented, they lost their fear of being penalized and began to enjoy school more.

High school students in one of my experimental settings were so negative and unpredictable that they had been bounced from public schools. Their communications were marred with frequent interruptions, rudeness, and ridicule.

Their teacher created a large chart. In columns across the top she listed eight communication skills with students' names down the side, and without explanation began giving them a tally mark for using a skill in class. They noticed quickly and began to congratulate themselves and then others. At first they did so jokingly, she said, but soon became serious about it. When she felt hurried and failed to record the tallies, the students asked her to continue them. When she allowed them to tally each other's use of skills, they complied enthusiastically, going to the chart at the end of small group work or during class discussions. She saw improvement in their personal relationships, communications, and sense of play. The approach is especially helpful when you risk rejection of a plan just because it comes from you. You might use these to start:

look at speaker
wait till other finishes
use others' names respectfully
use others' words and ideas respectfully
remember what others say
give compliments
thank people
tell what helped you

If you include your own name on the list, you encourage them to notice your modeling. Since the first two skills occur spontaneously as students interact with friends, the positive marks can accumulate quickly. Pause class, or say "When there's no more than one person there, you can go up and give anyone a tally." This can be tied to reward systems in lock-down schools or in classes for those with emotional or behavioral problems. Teachers and students can award tokens that are accumulated for prizes, food, or privileges.

Adapt for learning disabilities. Although many students with an identified disability are in special education classes, some in the mainstream still find an aspect of learning hard for them. This occurs most often in *getting the information inside them*. Once it's there, they may have superior retention and understanding. To make accessing easier, don't burden it with fluff. Ask them to learn only what you truly want them to keep, so that they don't work hard to learn what they'll discard anyway.

Find each one's open door and include it in the sequence everyone uses: see pictures of it, hear a description of it, write it down, speak it to a partner, speak it to the class, imagine it, repeat it, and give it structure. If you can include each one's strength in the format everyone uses, then all learn (26).

Deliver knowledge no faster than the pace at which they install it. 1) Transmit small segments written and summarized, 2) followed at once by Partner Practice to explain them, and 3) regular use of the Peg List to keep them fresh. Once they have a chunk inside them, reinforce it further by 4) Mental Movie and 5) Impromptu Performance, and 6) resynthesize it as new elements are added.

Individualized strategies may help. One for whom the physical act of writing is a barrier might for a time dictate to a parent or classmate, and another stands and acts out or symbolizes the material physically. Verbal expression means more to some. When they have more to learn than they can process, handouts and notes copied from other students may accommodate them.

CHAPTER 7

Replace Grading with Scoring

S cores are a way to record the successful completion of a unit of
students' effort. Here we examine problems with standard grading,
and how scoring by points of knowledge and time explaining can improve
the evaluation of students' progress and stimulate them.

43. Replace grading with scoring

Solving a problem usually depends on asking the right question. When
progress seems bogged down in a fitful struggle, we're encouraged to
examine our question.

Here we shift from the mass to the individual. We assume that federal,
state, and local authorities as well as parents and teachers all ultimately
want *what enables students to learn best*, so we ask that question first
instead of how we assess their learning. We look at one single student
and inquire, "Are we taking *this particular student* to the next step
of his or her *particular* learning sequence?" As the question is asked
millions of times per day across the country, the particular fulfills the
general need.

Attempting to define the student's effort with grades has proven
unsatisfactory (27). The reason this is inevitable is that *grades don't fix
learning at any consistent point on its trajectory from total ignorance
to complete mastery*. Imagine two students in different schools taking a
test on identical material. One faces a few multiple-choice and true-false
questions he answers in five minutes while the other must give a detailed
summary and evaluation of it piece by piece (with book closed) that takes
her forty-five minutes. Both qualify for an A grade, but it's not hard to guess
which is likely to know more. The fifteen steps below comprise what we
might call "Signals of the depth of knowledge." Teachers select among
them, telling the student "If you can do this step, I'll credit you." Lacking
a common standard, one believes steps four and five warrant an A grade
and another places it at step twelve.

1 **is present in class, sits still, and looks at you when you talk**
2 **recognizes "Yes, we had that!"**
3 **sorts a preposterous from a plausible answer**
4 **does sentence-completion and fill-in blanks**
5 **improves on fifty-fifty chance with a true-false answer**
6 **picks the right answer from a set of four**
7 **matches columns of associated terms**
8 **answers in a single word with coaching**
9 **answers in a single sentence with coaching**
10 **answers in a single sentence without help**
11 **gives a multi-part answer without help**
12 **comprehensively explains structure, terms, and details having just looked at the answer**
13 **gives answer 12 having last looked at it yesterday**
14 **gives answer 12 having last looked at it a week ago**
15 **gives answer 12 having last looked at it six months ago**

Learning relies on an impression in the mind that's carried forward or no learning occurs. If the mind must rely on the help that occurs in the first nine steps above, then it isn't carrying the learning forward under its own power, and the impressions in the mind are surface.

Scoring as I suggest it here is *a count of the student's increments of sustained success,* learning that has crossed the threshold of being independently retained by the mind and verified by the last six steps of the continuum. It presumes that trying to approximate the value of learning *before* that point is a waste of time; that what matters is what sticks, so we measure it when learning reaches at least that point and continue to hold it to that standard.

This is the essential activity in "nailing" learning. A student identifies a piece of knowledge, consciously practices and assimilates it, and goes on to another. With a piece clearly defined this way, he can count it, score it, claim it, post it, carry it forward, accumulate it, present it, and easily make it permanent by periodic attention to it (28).

Benefits from this kind of scoring are several. It **averts disputes.** Parents are less likely to complain about scores than about grades. A track and field score just says, "This is how high your child jumped," or "This is your child's time in the race." Period. We only want to represent accurately what he did: "Your child got twenty correct out of twenty-five." Period. It **focuses effort**. Scoring makes games both possible and appealing as an orderly, quick, objective summation of the effort involved. No need to trouble ourselves with how someone sees it. The score says it all, a platoon of influences brought to bear on one task. It's not a complete description of the skills drawn upon but is a marker of their excellence. We mobilize attention and determination, accomplish the task, achieve the score, and feel refreshed and satisfied. It brings effort **under students' control**, which applies from the recall of a single word to the mastery of a subject. Their points aren't compared to an abstract standard but correlate their effort directly with their progress without needing to please anyone, guess what others are thinking, or worry about how they're perceived. They just think "So far I got fifteen answers and I'm going for sixteen." They know exactly what their score is and others register it the same way. They experience **more freedom**. Nothing keeps them in a mould except the effort they expend. Scoring their ongoing work provides a tight feedback loop between intent and outcome even in ten minutes. Though their first score for an increment doesn't mean that they've mastered it yet, they've passed the crucial boundary of explaining it without help and can foresee continuing to meet the same criterion. If the knowledge disappears and the student can no longer explain it, the score drops proportionately. Scores present a **direct proportion** between the amount of effort, the amount of learning, and the resulting score. Effort lines up behind certified results and initial results grow to higher levels. Without accurate feedback about such details, energy along the continuum of effort loses aim, and verifiability of competence vanishes.

Instant scoring motivates more. Students are more ready for feedback about their efforts right after the effort is completed. Energy at its greatest receptivity is caught on the fly, so to speak, pointing them to their next burst of effort: "You got it! Now go on to the next." The motivational juice in the link between effort and results drops when validation of results is delayed. Once they mentally and emotionally leave their action behind, they must rely on other motives, and tend to accept belated approval indifferently. Immediate acknowledgment works differently. When someone says to us, "I'll check on you in a half hour," we work harder than we might otherwise. If they say, "I'll check on you at the end of the month," we tend to wait to exert the effort. Immediacy of feedback stimulates immediate effort. Specificity of scoring increases specific effort.

Scoring can accommodate **graded material.** If you continue to use grades instead of scoring quantities of knowledge mastered, you might post the number of answer points maintained till the end of the term that earn a grade. 300 points might be an A, 250 a B, and 200 a C. If you wish to use scoring primarily, you can still incorporate assignments that don't lend themselves to a score. Assigning a report for practice in researching, organizing, and writing, you might say "Your basic score for this term will be from the points and time of material you master. For this report, however, you'll be able to receive up to 100 points more, depending on the effort you put into it." You then assign their product a numerical score by how it meets your criteria.

44. Score by Points and Time

Points. Scoring by points presumes that much academic knowledge has discrete, equally challenging parts to learn: days of a week, 7; rules for commas, 11; names of muscles, 240. Each part is a specific chunk of knowledge. To assign points to knowledge not cleanly divided into parts, think of an essay question on a test. Grading it, you look for ideas you expect should be there, perhaps five or six. The score of the answer counts up points the answer supplies (in addition to other characteristics you wish to teach—cf. prior paragraph), and the student maintains the score by maintaining the answer.

In general we grant a point of score if a piece contains knowledge not made clear or explained elsewhere, with no half score for a half point. A point is a coherent thought expressed in a sentence or clause. Its size is determined by what readily hangs together at the class's level of understanding. A way to identify points is to think of what you consider mistakes. What could go wrong at this level is what to measure when it goes right. What you'd mark off as a mistake if missed on a test is an increment gained that deserves a score. As their work improves, something changes. Count the new thing that's added correctly.

Vague knowledge. Incomplete knowledge can be vague or partial. Vague is undefined. Students may "have the idea" enough to recognize it or guess at it, a kind of knowledge less useful to them.

Partial knowledge may still be boundaried, understood, and retained well though incomplete. It's credited as the number of sub-points told back correctly without help, such as four of seven. The four are definite, and the listener records this on the score line under or beside the question in the speaker's notebook and initials it. Partial knowledge points them toward completing the set while vague knowledge leaves them uncertain what to do next.

Assign scores to parts that are independently understood. To prepare for a trip to the airport, second graders learn parts of an airplane, naming those pointed out in a picture. The second stage is to tell the function of each part. Identifying and counting tells you the extent of the remaining task: "I have all seventeen parts named!" "Wonderful! Now learn what they do." Seventeen points learned, seventeen to go.

Students can help you. A high school student who caught on to this laid out the factoring of a polynomial in sixteen steps. "Is this what you had in mind?" he asked, and took me through the steps. Breaking a process into specific steps helps assure that each one is correct.

Score by time. Most students appear to be reassured by using points first because they define a task exactly, but many subjects are understood better through a narrative. Assembling scattered pieces into a coherent arrangement gives a better grasp of the whole. In literature, each step of a plot, literary element, or character analyzed can be learned as a point of knowledge but then scored further in an integrated explanation. The time they talk is a way to acknowledge their effort. A student caught onto using this measure, and I clocked him for nineteen minutes as he explained the chemistry of the sun from a TV special he'd seen the night before.

Time can measure mastery of many subjects that contain an abundance of details all equally valid to include. If your class studies the Civil War, one student may have a six minute explanation. A thirty-six minute student has read, practiced, and accumulated significant understanding. Then you discover a three hour and nineteen minute student who loves the subject and fascinates others.

One might ask why bother to time answers to the second. The reason is because it matters. It conveys unmistakably that "Even seconds of your knowledge *count*." They paid for it with their effort and would like to know their return on investment. A clue to the significance even of seconds is how our culture esteems quantified effort toward achievements possessing no intrinsic value. Most games and sports amount to an arbitrary way to combine effort and skill that become valued *because they can be measured*. We want to piggyback on this presumption by quantifying their explanations, yet to boot give them the intrinsic benefit of life knowledge. A compelling reason to adopt the scoring system suggested here is that it applies a mind-set that students already use extensively to authenticate their progress.

To reduce both forms into one score, **combine points and time at four points per minute** and express it either way. If in a week a student earns 36 points plus 16 minutes time, we multiply the minutes by 4 (based on the estimate that within a given minute, one speaks about 4 points of knowledge). In 16 minutes, one would cover 64 points: 16 x 4 = 64. Then we add these to the points already counted up: 64 + 36 = 100 points. To express the same score as time, we divide the 36 points by 4: 36 / 4 = 9, and add these to the timed minutes: 9 + 16 = 25 minutes score.

If time is used alone, ask them to get the answer smoothly in mind before presenting it to a partner for scoring. You might introduce a subject and have students practice it initially on Monday. They re-explain it on Tuesday, and score it for the record on Wednesday. If repetition, hesitance, vagueness, or padding with irrelevant information occurs, listeners can take off an appropriate amount of the score.

Personal characteristics can influence timing, so that students' scores for the same material may not match exactly. Some talk slower and some faster. Some with many words say a little and others use few words to say a lot. The adult world values both elaboration and conciseness, and we want students able to do either. What matters is how a change in their score reveals effort to accumulate fresh knowledge while maintaining the prior.

As students add new material to old answers, they can insert new sheets in their notebooks at the appropriate places. If the new material doesn't alter the form of what's there already that they know well, they can increase their score for that question without re-telling the previous material.

Standardize the recording of questions. The notebook arrangement helps you know each question's stage of development; first that it's complete with all the pieces correct, and later that it's permanent. Scoring focuses practice by telling how much of the information has reached the criterion of explainability-without-help.

Let's say that in Language Arts a student has been reading *War and Peace:*
24. What's the story of *War And Peace* by Tolstoy?
4:30t LB/ 19:10t TL/ 1:32:43t AS
The score line says that in his first attempt at summarizing the book, listener L.B. timed him for four and a half minutes. His second attempt was nineteen minutes and ten seconds, timed by student T.L. His third attempt, after he read to the end of the book, was timed by a student or family member with the initials A.S. for an hour and thirty-two minutes and forty-three seconds. For adapting practice to the shorter times available in a classroom, you might divide a book into separate questions about chapters, plot line, key events, philosophy expressed, cultural and environmental elements, character development, and relationships between characters.

In the sciences, questions 32, 73, and 74 might appear as:
32. Define 13 terms related to fish on page 350 of Life Science text [13].
9p KS/ 13p LT
For questions scored by points, the bracketed numbers at the end of a question tell the number of points in a complete answer if it's known so that the student knows the point of task completion. At first, he or she could recite nine of thirteen terms to someone with the initials K.S. and was credited with nine points. Later to a listener initialed L.T., the student demonstrated mastery of all of them.
73. Name and explain ten factors that affect the climate [10].
5p PR/ 8p KS/ 10p KS
After this student gathered the ten factors answering the question, he told back five of them to another initialed P.R. Student K.S. heard eight and then ten on two occasions. In the next question the student might draw on the same information with a narrative explanation for an added score:
74. Explain the circulation of the atmosphere.
:30t RG/ 1:45t FL/ 3:10t AS
The student incorporated some of the information from question 73 into question 74, and expanded it to 3 minutes 10 seconds after initially

explaining it for a half-minute. The presence of the colon (and absence of "p" for points) indicates a timed answer, or students may wish to add a "t" for clarity.

49. Give three rules and examples for order of operations [6].

3p RT/ 4p AS/ 6p LT

This score might indicate any combination of rules and examples that totaled three at first, then four, then all six possible.

If a question arises about what time score to apply to a portion of learning, be guided by the effort involved. If they wish to score a new piece that appears to you a retooling of something already learned, ask "What new effort resulted in this learning?" For more examples of scoring by points, see 54.

Clarify level of detail. It often happens that as they practice explaining a section, their answers become shorter. They're more efficient with the same knowledge. Account for this as a sign that they're achieving mastery, that a competent person can recast knowledge, talking either at length or with a brief summary depending on the situation. To standardize an explanation so that it renders a consistent score, grade school students appreciate a guideline. Your own words are one model: "Say what I would in presenting it, along with diagrams, examples, and illustrations." Or, "Think how you'd tell it to a younger brother or sister so they could understand it." Or you might suggest, "If a new person came to class who didn't know this material and you were assigned to help him catch up, what would you say?"

If they can demonstrate a masterful explanation in less time than previously measured, there's no need to reduce their score, however, unless it represents knowledge lost. We assume that most could use up extra words to fill time if they needed to.

45. Points Scoreboard

Because we wish never to embarrass or discourage students, we weigh carefully the stresses we place upon them. We don't want to gather information about them in a way that diminishes what they learn. The most motivational way to measure their progress, we conclude above, is to count up the increments they master. Here we weigh the degree of public recognition to give to their scores, even posting their hourly progress on a classroom chart (cf. Appendix 7). We have two models to choose from.

In one, the student achieves and is acknowledged. This occurs in a myriad of activities, particularly individual and team sports, competitions, and electronic games. When a number representing their effort appears, their body language tells their pleasure. They're glad to have their accomplishment known, win or lose. They understand that it's fair, that it can change over time and often quickly, measures something they have control over; and that they're not helpless in the face of a teacher's attitude, nor set aside because they're of a different race or academic status, nor zeroed out by others more capable. Their achievement has its own substance that they can increase by more effort.

The other model is that of a student being judged. Because the judgment is someone's opinion, it responds less directly to their effort and can leave them feeling diminished. A child's "spin" on how their score is treated can create comfort or discomfort. Several factors might influence them.

1. Does the system continue something already familiar? Starting from kindergarten (cf. 32. Primary Grades), we can use scoring to convey complete success for everyone for as long as that matters to them. If some take a little longer to achieve it, no matter; and if some add more points, that's fine too.

2. Does the scoreboard give them information they can use? The Content Scoreboard (cf. 47) helps them monitor their accumulated learning, gain clues from how others pursue their tasks, and make personal choices about where to direct their effort.

3. Is the score under their control? It should be the direct outcome of their effort rather than someone's judgment about them. Their practice increases their knowledge in exact proportion to their effort.

4. Is the score accurate? We want a reliable reflection of their effort.

5. Is it comparative or personalized? Comparative scores may stimulate those of roughly equal ability but discourage those too different. As their posted scores vary for mastering the same material, the teacher can explain a basic fact about life:

   Let's say two students are reading. One finds three points she wants to save, and writes them down and practices them in order to master them. Another reads for awhile, finds one point he wants to save, and thinks about it a lot. Then he writes it down and practices it to save it. Are the three points better than the one point? (Let them think about it and offer their views.) **Really, we don't know. The point the second student saves may be very valuable to him later. He may call on it often in his lifetime, and the first student may drop the three points soon. We don't know the value of the points. The scores just help each one keep track of their own progress. They know how much more knowledge they have today than yesterday, but how they use it later is up to them. What we want from each one now is just that they learn something well. They'll choose later how valuable it becomes to them.**

6. Is it group-oriented or individual? Often students are motivated to increase a team score. If your Tuesday goal for the class is six points apiece for each of twenty students, they might be spurred to reach the overall goal of 120 points total. You monitor and post their collective achievement. Students know their contribution to it question by question but are stimulated by a group focus on a larger target.

7. Is it the only way they're recognized? Children come to understand that there are different abilities, that no one is good at everything. One average in academics may excel in communication skills, and one great in music isn't good at building things. Throughout their lives they'll encounter differences in skills, so it's realistic for them to know that competences vary and that this is okay.

8. Are they expending effort? Children draw from what they sense you truly believe. If you're confident that what counts day to day is their effort on tasks that build overall accomplishment and that they benefit from an objective record of it, that's what they'll believe too. Convey to them your conviction that their progress is not a matter of ability or opinion, but of steady effort.

If they're old enough to understand research information, tell them about Professor K. Anders Ericsson of Florida State University. He was curious about what separated people at the top of their field from others. The difference wasn't in intelligence, he found. The IQ of those at the top of their field typically matched that of the average college student. What set them apart instead was that they put in thousands of hours more practice than did average performers in their field. It held true that "practice made perfect" (29). Tell your students about the tortoise and the hare. What matters is that they persevere. Let them know accurately how they're doing by means of objective scores, and provide a clear map for altering their results.

Name	Monday	Tuesday	Wednesday	Thursday	Friday	Total
Jill	15	8	9	14	20	(66)
Bill						
Will						
Phil						

The Points Scoreboard design above works well when scoring with points only, but if time is used also, the two are coalesced into a single point score daily till Friday when they're added into the cumulative total. Jill's scores through the week add up to 66. Students may turn in their points hour by hour or at the end of the day, as the teacher prefers, and someone is assigned to post the scores. When the total is recorded, the numbers that went into it are erased.

Maintain the standard that only real numbers are worth posting, scores *verified by their partner for specific questions the student can answer.* Monitor their accuracy by listening in while students explain them, by employing Impromptu Performance frequently, and by switching partners.

46. Mastery Scoreboard

The Mastery Scoreboard below accommodates the use of both points and time. Across the top, label columns as daily and cumulative time, daily and cumulative points, and a combined total expressed as either points or time (cf. Appendix 7).

Names	Daily Points	Cumulative Points	Daily Time	Cumulative Time	Combined Total
Fred	13	25	2:40	10: 22	70 points
Red					
Jed					
Ted					

At the end of a period or day, students report to you on a slip of paper 1) their name, 2) the number of points or time they gained, and 3) the name of the student who signed off on their count. Daily points can either be added to the total throughout the day or penciled on the chart separately each hour (e.g. 4, 8, 3, 10) and then added at the day's end. Erase scores from a prior column when you combine them in a cumulative or total column. See 44. for how Fred's scores in the accompanying chart are converted.

If you don't have acetate over the chart, enter scores with a large soft-lead pencil easy to erase. Make a matching one for your personal notebook in case someone tampers with the scoreboard or enters incorrect numbers.

Students enjoy posting their scores. Soon after introducing her class to it, a high school teacher said to me, "We're charting all kinds of things now!"

More visibility makes their effort more significant. A principal might ask for a matching scoreboard from each room to display in a central hallway, or classes might post there a single line chart for their total progress in learning, all individual scores added together.

47. Content Scoreboard

Besides displaying scores, scoreboards can organize content.

Elementary. In elementary classes, post a large erasable version of the blank chart in Appendix 6. Teach the comma and semi-colon, for example, by writing each use at the head of a column with student names down the side. When a student learns one of the uses, place an X in that column beside his/her name. When everyone learns the entire series, erase it and insert a different learning task, dividing its parts among the column headings. As their pace picks up, cycle the content daily, tracking any subject with answers organized into parts they can cross off as they learn them one by one. They have a visual record of their progress as they master each step.

High School. Let's say you're a biology teacher with a 700 page text of twenty-six chapters and you want to increase their total knowledge about biology. While you have a few priorities you insist on, you welcome anything at all that they learn from the book.

Make an erasable wall chart. Write a chapter number in each of the columns across the top and student names down the side. Students then maintain a count of all the points they learn in answer to all the questions they draw from each chapter. By requiring nothing more than that they maintain their point scores to the end of the term, you make much permanent learning likely.

Chapter Name	1	2	3	4	5	6	7	8	///	26
Bill	29	23	9	6	19	1	5	4		7
Phil										
Will										

Visible scores invite them to fill in gaps. Scanning his scores above, Bill notices that he has only one point in Chapter 6, and decides that in the minutes remaining till the end of a period he might pick up more. He reads briefly, writes notes on his Answers page, records a question, and has two more points in Chapter 6 on track to mastery.

Encourage students to proceed into any chapter that interests them and share what they get with others. This helps familiarize them with the subject's structure, allows them to shift focus for the sake of variety, matches the non-linear way most people follow an interest over time, and gives them social capital by knowing something others are likely to value.

Tracking remedial work. The Content Scoreboard can help you monitor remedial work if students are assigned to you from different courses. Make twelve to fifteen columns. When students arrive, signing their name on the first open line tells them they're going to accumulate scores about doable tasks. Head the first five columns:

1   **Mission**
2   **Appreciation**
3   **Communication**
4   **Life Knowledge**
5   **Study Methods**

Number the remaining ones six and up. For each subject they need to practice in your class, they designate a column for their scores on it. One might tally science scores in a column another uses for math.

The first column invites you to develop a mission statement describing what you direct them to do. Remember the axiom *If you don't know where you're going, you'll probably end up somewhere else.* Your concept about your mission organizes everything that occurs in your class. One that fits the present design is "to help ourselves and each other learn as much as possible as enjoyably as possible." Discuss your mission with them and give them a score of "1" on the chart when they can tell it back. Return to it periodically for their assessment of how well they apply it. For the content of columns 2-5, draw on the relevant sections of this book and other methods adapted to your students.

48. Language and Math

The exactness inherent in language and math invites precise methods of instruction. Here we focus just on how to account for the gains made.

Accommodate precision. Most mathematical and scientific processes involve specific formulas, definitions, and steps easily divided into points of knowledge. And in languages, we can count as a point each vocabulary word or sentence translated; each grammar rule and different verb or noun form. Many nouns and verbs in foreign languages have regular forms of declension or conjugation, so more points aren't awarded for repeating the same forms. They don't deserve an additional score unless they required more learning effort.

In both math and languages, we find many instances of a single point of knowledge applied to diverse contexts—think of a math formula or a set of vocabulary or a grammar rule. Learning the main point means mastering a representative sampling of its variant applications. I refer to the number needed as a *mastery count*, the alternate forms mastered that brings the point of knowledge to the competence desired, the items needed in a set for students to comprehend its unifying principle. This differs slightly from assigning students pages of problems that they learn uncertainly. However many they practice, *they need at least a few that they master perfectly.* This might mean working a given number of problems with different data, or noting several instances that generalize an idea. Several dozen examples might generalize a math process or perhaps five uses of a foreign language word establish its broader meaning. Babies seem able to learn the word for a given object on hearing three uses of it.

While your school's foreign language curriculum may limit you to a form for each lesson, you can create your own expanding system to link associated meanings with appropriate variation. In putting several words into different foreign language sentences, award a point for each sentence that changes at least one word, up to a limit of five. In the sentence "I like chocolate," for example, change the word "chocolate" to "lemonade," "orange juice," "tea," and "coffee." Five alternates complete the main idea, "I like (to drink something)," and the term is given its maximum of five points. Each of those sentences then can be altered in four other ways using the words associated with them. "I like coffee" invites adjectives like "hot," "cold," "fresh," "strong." and verbs such as "drink," "pour," and "taste." Each new adjective or verb inserted into an already-familiar sentence is a new point of knowledge. Using a word in three to five different combinations usually provides the mind a sufficient base, although often-used words with many distinct meanings may need a larger mastery count.

Mastery of a single math principle typically incorporates knowledge from several angles. A teacher may ask a student to complete a set of three to five problems and explain them in summary, with the score for the overall answer including a point for each of the following:

definition of terms such as "area" and "trapezoid."
purpose the principle is used for
any condition or assumption involved in using it
formula given
each step of a problem-solving sequence
examples of problem-solving with real numbers (up to three)
part of a whole if the function is a portion of something else
practical applications that might occur later

Incorporating such details, a comprehensive answer to a math question might include over a dozen points of knowledge. Even if you ask students to do many problems to practice a formula, select just three for them to explain with accurate words and integrated knowledge and record in their notebook (as though they were a teacher explaining the subject to younger students using their notebook as text).

And one more time, why bother? Why measure gains in knowledge at such a micro-level? For an answer, remember all the ways quantitative improvement is measured and rewarded in society today, apply those reasons to classroom effort, and watch how students' learning and satisfaction change.

49. Reading

Sir Francis Bacon summed up the language skills students need: "Reading makes a full man, writing an exact man, and conference (conversation) a ready man." We want students full of valid knowledge but more often overhear banal conversations that rehash a limited world.

Reading is their antidote, drawing them into the larger human condition and expanding their range of words and ideas. It's reasonable just to let them choose what interests them, give them time to read, and hope they'll enjoy it. Some schools start the day with a "sacred" half hour of reading that nothing else may interrupt, presuming that just by steady reading they can't help but improve.

We might hope also for conscious learning from what they read. We want for them a refined internal model of all that human experience contains, and encourage this by providing them a way to express what they absorb. Saying "You're tutoring about this tomorrow" gives them an expectation to act. They think about the material differently, grasp it more deeply, and incorporate new ideas better. We want an action set in their mind: "You're going to do a stand-up report about this tomorrow," or "When you're done reading, explain to your partner what you read," or "Now tell the story." A tangible reason spurs them to lace pieces together. Unless they do this soon after they read, their later attempt to do so is certain to be less coherent.

Social meaning of knowledge. While you may ask them to extract Q and A from their reading, even exchanging brief comments about it has power beyond the minutes devoted to it. *It activates the social role of knowledge.* We enhance their reading by wiring it into their social needs, turning it into a vehicle for personal relationships.

Arrange them in pairs, each one reading something different. Ask them to pause after, say, ten minutes of reading and in a few sentences summarize to each other what they've read. Arrange twenty percent of their reading time to express it to a partner, or end a fifty minute reading period with "Tell your stories back and forth for five minutes each." Their reading gains immediate relevance when they use it to connect with someone and find that they "have something going" with this person they didn't know before. Reading they can talk about is a doorway to being accepted and validated, giving them an incentive to read well, and tell in detail what they find.

Narrating knowledge as a story helps them integrate it. Assign them to find out who these people were who wrote this, and why they say these things. The sciences become more interesting this way, how someone met a challenge by following out an idea. Math concepts stick better when incorporated into their historical development with personalities, events, and conditions. Story and background together are a richer feast for the imagination and more likely to be drawn on later. For variety use Mental Movie between their reading and their telling of it, and improve the quality of their exchange further with a half-minute reviewing communication skills before and after.

A brief use of time is to ask them to write in their notebooks just one question about what they read and a telegraphic answer to it. Even a minute a day at this helps them retain more. They can also talk later to a Designated Listener about their reading (cf. 31).

50. Writing

With students expressing to someone else what they read and building their social capital, we can generate an Amazon of thought. Next we hone its expression, bringing their writing up to basic competence. It becomes easier as they read and talk readily, so we first open their word flow. For two weeks, after their daily reading but before they share it with partners, tell them, "Think for a minute about what you're going to say about what you've read." When they realize they can put words to their ideas consciously, shift the means of expression: "Today instead of saying it, just write it down" like they would speak it word by word. (Some may benefit by dictating to a partner.)

When they can express a stream of ideas in a rough draft, shift emphasis to its mechanics. Help them revise with guidelines that make it clear, efficient, and eventually elegant. If you can, arrange for older students to give one on one encouragement. The best inspiration for pushing the edge of nearly any ability often comes from students slightly older.

From you, they most need individualized feedback. Each change you suggest is for them a new point of knowledge. You convey it as a positive point of learning rather than as a mistake, and credit them with a score as they can explain it back to you. Keep your own computerized listing of the changes you expect from each student, and require them to apply it in their future writing to maintain the score. At the rate of just five corrections per paper on one paper a week, in a school year they accumulate 180 improvements. What's critical is continuing to use them, making the corrections permanent once understood.

CHAPTER 8

Demonstrate Learning

O nce students are confident of their knowledge, they need ways to demonstrate it to each other, to parents, and to the educational system. Here we suggest a summary report of their learning and several ways to perform it before others.

51. Academic Mastery Report

Collect the results of their learning practice in a regularly updated, individual Academic Mastery Report. Add up the total explaining time or number of points they've achieved for each unit or section in every course and subject. Produce it weekly for special needs students and at least monthly for others. For students seriously demoralized, consider having them handwrite and update their report at the end of each day:

Look at each section in your notebook. Find the questions you could answer, and list the number of points under each one that you can tell back by the end of the day without help. Add up all those points. Under Science, you'll remember, we dealt with worms and I put four points on the board. If you've told back all four points, write *Science: worms (4p)*. In math, we had fractions and covered eight points. If you got five of them by the end of the day, you could write *Math: fractions (5p)*. In Literature, maybe you learned four lines of the poem and four other things we discussed about poetry, so write *Literature: poetry (8p)*.

On subsequent days they add to totals in existing categories, and you start new ones. If any wish to include personal interests or a unique expertise, have a parent or other student listen to them, score their explanation by time or points, and sign off on it.

The primary accounting work is theirs. You teach the points you want retained, and they do everything else—master them, count them, and record totals. You might also find someone—a school employee, older student, parent, or other volunteer—who'll update their reports. Gather the week's data by Friday for the volunteer to process over the weekend, and send them home or email them on Monday.

Because each digit represents a success, matches their effort perfectly, and describes learning they own and can demonstrate anytime, students are pleased to erase old scores, incorporate increases, show their results to their parents, and maintain them. The report helps sustain their pride and continued effort.

ACADEMIC MASTERY REPORT
For
Melissa Lewis, XYZ High School, 2006-2007.

BIOLOGY: biology basics (59p), chemical compounds (16p), cells, DNA, life basics (85p), evolution (20p), classification and earth's beginnings (19p); bacteria, viruses (33p); algae, fungi, ferns (29p), seed plants (38p). Total 299 points.

RUSSIAN: declensions (85p), conjugations (70p), grammar rules (32p), vocabulary (933p), sentences (214p), dialogs (93 min). Total 1357 points, 1 hour 33 minutes.

MATH: definitions of terms (193p), algebraic rules (114p), demonstration problems (350p), problem-solving steps (745p), applications (487p). Total 1889 points.

US HISTORY: place names (163p), names and terms in military conflicts (189p), important people (91p); political, social, and cultural terms (111p), historical narrative 1600-1850 (27:10), Civil War era 1850-1865 (43:22), rebuilding South 1865-1900 (22:35), industry and expansion to 1900 (32:12), politics and protest to 1900 (29:51), Progressive Movement to 1920 (39:17), World War I (20:19), Depression and New Deal (27:23). Total 554 points, 4 hours 2 minutes.

GEOGRAPHY: place names (231p), terms (188p), maps (177p), earth surface (39p), climate/vegetation (47p), population (29p), culture (32p), North America (27p), Latin America (52p), Europe (67p), Russia and eastern Europe (51p), Africa and SW Asia (44p), SE Asia (31p), Australia and polar (36p). Total 1051 points.

WRITING: corrected errors (38p), principles of composition (29p), grammar rules (19p), personal journal (2,555 words), field logbook (667 words), reports for classes (1,116 words), first draft writing (1,982 words), edited writing (3,825 words), poetry (775 words). Total 86 points and 10,920 words written.

TOTALS. Points: 299, 1357, 1889,554, 1051, 86=5,236 points. Time 5 hours 35 minutes. Writing: 10,920 words.

CERTIFICATION: this is to certify that we, ___John Smith___ and ___Adam Smith___, questioned this student for (length of time) ___two hours___ on (date) ___June 16, 2007___, drawing questions randomly from the original records of the summary above. Our finding is that this student knew (percent) ___98%___ of the knowledge claimed.

DATE: ___June 17, 2007___   SIGNED ___*John Smith*___
                                                         SIGNED ___*Adam Smith*___

---

52. Curriculum Performance

A **topic performance** is a formal public speaking event in which students present one or more Learning Feats they've mastered. It becomes more significant as the audience expands.

Arrange for a room to accommodate student performers and their guests. If your options are a space larger than you need or one that's a tight fit, go with the smaller. A crowded room increases emotional impact.

Limit their offerings to a length all can perform in an evening presentation. Print a program listing each one's topic, time, and room number, and give them a supply to distribute to their relatives and neighbors. Everyone they invite increases their motivation to prepare. Get students working quietly and go on the phone to parents, complimenting their child's preparation for the event.

On the assigned day, students and parents go to their assigned rooms. Students are called on as scheduled, rise to give their performance, accept applause, acknowledge it till it dies down, and return to their seats. A brief award ritual dignifies their achievement and boosts pride. A certificate might contain the student's name, the date, and a description of their feat such as "Described ten animals found on Mount Kilimanjaro," or "Explained the historical development of geometry," or "Described how to clean a fish." Provide refreshments and a socializing time. At home, parents can affix the certificate to the wall and say, "We were there when you did that."

A **curriculum performance** draws on the entire curriculum thus far. One way to arrange it is **top twenty,** a set of inclusive questions larger than the number of students in the class that potentially draw on most or all of their learning. The questions need not be the same for everyone. Each writes out their personal list of major performable questions and turns it in to you. Place counters in a bag up to the agreed-on number of questions.

Draw students' names randomly, and as they advance to the front of the room, a member of the audience (perhaps one of their guests) draws a counter. You look at the student's list and ask the question corresponding to that number (or any next in sequence that hasn't already been asked), creating a game-like atmosphere with an element of chance. The student answers one or more questions up to the time allotted.

In this design students prepare twenty or more talks to give instead of a single one as in a topic performance. Few answer exactly the same question, so differences in ability are muted. Each receives celebration, and the emotional dynamic is the same for all.

A second design is to ask students to write on separate slips every individual question they can answer and place them in an **individual bag**. They can accumulate a substantial fund of such questions by adding a few every day that they practice in Impromptu Performances. At the public event, as they proceed to the front of the room, someone draws a slip from their bag and asks the question written on it, skipping those duplicating one asked already. The student speaks for the time allotted (one answer might take twenty-five seconds, another two minutes, and a third a minute and a half).

Award certificates can acknowledge students' entire Learning Feat total from which selection is made instead of the few they perform: "Demonstrated mastery of ninety-two minutes of Learning Feats from five subjects." Eight minutes performing may validate ninety-two minutes of learning just as a few test questions do for ten times as many that weren't asked. When awards are presented, each receives a description of their feat read aloud, a certificate handed to them, and applause.

53. Checkpoint Morning

To guarantee learning, hold students to a mastery-producing task till they produce mastery.

Checkpoint Morning is a way to do this for upper elementary or older, or for self-contained classes that are together for two or three hours. It spurs selecting, organizing, recording, mastering, and performing learning while incorporating both student freedom and teacher control of results. Students demonstrate that they can explain something without help for a measured time.

Guide the experience firmly and insist on results. If your class already sets to work at what you ask of them, they don't need the reward activity, but you may wish to provide one anyway. If many underperform, or unhappy feelings divide them, or they lack discipline and concentration, a reward may jump-start them into cooperating. Ideally it should be something they can turn to right away when they complete the task, or a larger one toward which they can accumulate points. Options might be the use of valued school facilities such as computers, audio-visual or exercise equipment, or watching a video. They might play quiet games one-to-one, or (if you can gain permission to allow them some freedom) go to a gym or playground or other activities within school rules. You might consider also a reward that totals up points as a group: "When we get a hundred minutes of mastered learning from everyone together, we'll have a game-hour instead of class." Discuss what appeals to them that's feasible in your setting.

With the reward understood, you need only a room rich in resources, a kitchen timer or a clock with a visible second hand, and a list of the students with space by their names for recording their accomplishment. Say to them:

> **You're going to have an interesting experience this morning. From any of your texts or other sources here in the room, I want you to find something of interest to learn** (or specify the subject matter as you wish). **When you have a minute's worth of learning from it, you'll teach it to someone else. As you read, just think, "How would I explain this?" When your explanation runs at least a minute, arrange it as question and answer. Write out at the top of your notes the question or questions you've chosen and your answer below. What you can say in a minute is about a page of writing, so aim for that and then time it. When you have your questions and answers written, trade yours with someone else. You each copy the other's, and then together learn both your own and the other person's. Explain them back and forth to each other until you both know both answers. When you and your partner have learned at least two minutes worth, come to me and let me hear it. Show me your written record and be able to talk for two minutes without repeating yourself. When you've done that, you're free to go to the activity we agreed on.**

Help those needing assistance to find a topic. They read for ten to thirty minutes, write down a question and its extended answer, and then find someone else. They sit together, trade papers, copy down what the other gathered, ask questions to understand it, and practice explaining both papers back and forth. When they feel ready to face your checking, they approach you and demonstrate their knowledge. Having their notes in front of you, you needn't hear the whole two minutes, but can spot check details as you wish. A few work intensively for thirty minutes so they can begin the reward activity you arranged. Everyone goes at their own pace and you monitor and aid as needed. In doing these things, they

> **survey their own interests**
> **practice research skills**
> **talk about ideas**
> **organize them as question and answer**
> **summarize them in writing**

relate to another student by exchanging learning
install knowledge in short-term memory
exert some self-discipline
follow directions
initiate a system for accumulating learning

Everyone succeeds and feels more connected to someone else so predictably that you have the features of a guarantee. You can assure learning because you can send them back for more work if they're short of the two minutes, a step more significant if they goofed off and must stay behind while their friends receive the reward activity. If some don't produce the two minutes by the end of the morning, in essence you make them a deal. Since they can't use "freedom leading to results," you switch to "control leading to results." The following day they sit beside you and work under your direct oversight.

If you wish to continue the design, the second day with the same instructions you ask them also to retain their prior learning. As they add more day by day, they're likely to improve at using their time, and you can modify what you ask of them: "By the end of the week, learn something from math, American literature, and science." They're accountable for results but with many free choices. They originate their own progress, work at their own pace, and expand their knowledge while you act as their consultant about the subject matter and monitor the activity.

54. Silver Bullet Team Competition

Competing at almost any activity tends to give it energy but most school competitions advance winners and exclude the less skilled who most need the support of a team experience. The design here includes everyone, and builds on scoring points of knowledge as explained above. Three stages provide different levels of challenge.

STAGE ONE

The simplest involves a single classroom. Small teams master knowledge in a short time and submit to questioning by an opposing team.

1. *Object of the competition.* Students work together in small groups to learn all they can in three to five days. You can specify a subject or let them add to all their courses. Their effort in preparing is the main benefit of the competition, stimulated by the prospect of accounting for it to each other.

2. *Participants.* To make teams balanced in ability, list each student's current total of scored learning to date. Combine them to make team totals as equal as possible while spreading out class leaders. You might consult students' suggestions for composing teams or see

18. Organization Groups for a way to do this. An even number of teams makes competition easier, and an even number of members on each team makes their practice sessions easier though most classes involve some mix of teams of four, five, or six members.

Different ability levels may have separate leagues (think Special Olympics) but within a given grade, team composition should even out the presence of students' uncommon ability. Three bright students might help one who's less accomplished and create a great experience for everyone. Emphasize the equality of the team totals at the start.

3. *Concentration Time.* After identifying teams, plan several days during which they can spend most or all of their time preparing for the competition. Call it "Concentration Time." Each team works together either to expand their answers on any questions they've learned before or add new ones. Following your guidance about the content you want, they locate and organize new information in clear notes, teach it to each other, and share their notes for others to photocopy or write out. When they add to existing notes, they mark where the new competition material begins.

4. *The Exchange.* Thirty minutes before match time, opposing teams exchange copies of the questions team members can answer that they've learned during Concentration Time. Teams examine their opponents' lists to decide what questions they want to ask of specific members of the other team. The judge appointed for the meet—preferably a teacher or older student familiar with the students' knowledge—determines that the learning is valid for their grade level.

5. *The Meet.* Matches between teams can be drawn randomly on meet day. Schedule them into different rooms of the school before their own judge, parents, and visitors. Two ways of judging teams that have different numbers of members are 1) for the judge to weigh the *average* per-student knowledge gained on each team, or 2) for the larger team to sideline one or more members by drawing straws.

Before each round, place the names of its members in a team bag, and from one team draw a point student who answers questions, and from the other a questioner. The point student gives his/her answer material to the judge.

All questions addressed to the point student go through the questioner. Others on the questioning team help by passing notes, whispering, or pointing to questions they think would be good to ask next.

The same length of questioning time for everyone is set by the teacher, between three and six minutes. Questioning probes any weaknesses in the point student's claimed knowledge. Once the questioner feels she's uncovered the strength of an answer, she can interrupt the point student by saying "Thank you" and asking a different question.

The judge weighs the total knowledge the student claims to have gained during Concentration Time by how well he/she responds to the specific questions asked, and assigns an overall percent score that affirms how much of what was asked was known. Five minutes of competent answers might validate fifty minutes of learning claimed.

When the student's questioning is completed, the direction of questioning switches. A name is drawn for a point student from the other team, and a questioner from the team that just answered. Previous participants are given a rest unless they're the last on their team to fill the role.

6. *Final Score.* When all students have been questioned, the judge decides which team obtained the most new mastered answers during Concentration Time, and names the winner. For a more exact score, the judge can

   1) total together all the points of knowledge each student on the team claims to have added during Concentration Time, and

   2) multiply that number of points by the average percent that students on that team demonstrated they knew during the questioning.

   If the judge rates two students at 90% and two at 80%, the team's rating is 85%. The total knowledge all the team members claim to have mastered is then multiplied by 85% and the highest resulting team score wins. (For comparison, see Appendix 10, the Individual Match Worksheet that's used with Stage Three, but here without the calculation for each separate question).

7. *Next Meet.* They maintain the same team composition for succeeding meets if their skills in the first one are comparable enough that outcomes are uncertain and winning depends on their effort. If teams are clearly uneven, develop new ones unless they're already so cohesive that all members would rather stay together. If you have any doubt, ask for anonymous written feedback.

STAGE TWO

This extends the prior design. The meet and scoring are the same except:

1. Teams may be from more than one classroom or school.

2. Concentration Time isn't used.

3. All learning is welcome including personal interests, hobbies, books read, special areas of expertise, prior or additional work for any course, and the entire year's curriculum to date. Students need only separate their material into question and answer, score it by time or points, and organize it in writing well enough that a judge can follow it.

4. Because of the larger quantity of learning involved, the time between the exchange and the meet is longer, allowing perhaps an hour or more for teams to prepare the questions they'll ask of their opponents.

5. The judge declares which team demonstrates the largest quantity of learning overall. If teams have an unequal number of members, they're compared on the basis of average per-student score (total learning divided by the number of students on the team) after the calculation explained in point 6 above.

STAGE THREE

Scores are determined as accurately as possible, and the outcome is based partly on how teams use skill and judgment during the meet.

Stage Three accommodates inter-school competition involving numerous teams and two or more upper elementary, middle, or high schools. The teams submit to each other the Learning Feats they've mastered, challenge each other's claimed knowledge, scoring shifts back and forth as questions validate or find weakness in a score claimed, and winners are determined. Comprehensive material can be included, and judging is more precise. In more detail:

Specific terms refer to features of the competition.

Students develop a clear question and answer summary of everything they know.

Team members help each other expand their knowledge.

They assign a score of points or time for each answer.

Remote Preparation
1. **The Focus**
2. **Team Makeup**
3. **Team Practices**

Learning Format
4. **Learning Feat List (ILF)**
5. **Total Team Challenge (TTC)**
6. **Long Answers**
7. **Short Answers**
8. **The 5-Second Rule**

Final Preparation
9. **The Checkout**
10. **The Exchange**
11. **The Strategy Session**
12. **Risk/Reward**

The Meet
13. **The Setting**
14. **The Questioning**
15. **Completeness Criteria**

Judging
16. **Judges**
17. **Scoring**
18. **Outcomes**
19. **Inter-School Meets**

Individual Match Worksheet

Answer lengths are sectioned to include learning of any quantity.

Competing teams exchange a complete list of the questions their members can answer.

Students question each other in one-to-one matches.

A judge rates the point student question by question.

A scoring team converts the ratings to team scores.

Points taken from one team during the meet are awarded to the other.

The team ending with the highest point total is the winner.

Changes in score are posted as the match proceeds.

The rules are listed here in sections (cf. box).

REMOTE PREPARATION

1. *The Focus.* The benefit of a specific focus for a meet is the greater depth of study and conversation it generates among team members. Organizers can leave the focus open to all knowledge or limit it to a subject such as math, science, or history. As desired, it can include both curricular and personal interest material; scientific or nature-related programs on video or television; and regional, ethnic, and cultural matters. Issues of public concern, economics, and world conditions can be timely. If no focus is predetermined, it's assumed that all knowledge arranged according to the criteria below is eligible.

2. *Team Makeup.* Competing classrooms or schools divide entire classes into teams of equal ability, each team a representative mix of the students of that grade level (cf. Stage One, 2. Participants). Using an even number (four or six if possible) makes pairing easier during team practices.

3. *Team Practices.* Practice sessions of an hour can be scheduled during or after the class day. Team members prepare to recall and explain everything they know, organizing and mastering all schoolwork well enough to relate it readily to a questioner. Middle and high schools could designate Learning Competition a separate course for mastering other courses. In the practices, team members 1) bring information they've collected and made notes on, 2) add each other's material to their own list of questions and answers, 3) write out answers they develop together, 4) help each other understand and explain all the learning they collect, 5) invent strategies for remembering it more easily, and 6) verify and sign off on each other's times and points.

LEARNING FORMAT

4. *Individual Learning Feat (ILF) List.* A Learning Feat is a chunk of learning arranged as a question and answer, and timed (or points

of knowledge counted) by a listening partner. Team practices result in increases to students' ILF lists, lengthening the times of prior feats or adding new ones. The length of the answering time (or the number of new points of knowledge) attained is noted under each question beside the initials of the person checking it. Some examples:

Describe the ten largest rivers in the world. 9:45t JE = 9 minutes 45 seconds of time verified by student J.E.

Explain five principles of geometry. 5:13t LS = 5 minutes 13 seconds of time verified by student L.S.

Compare politics before the American Revolution with today's. 6:00t FM, 11:16t CS = 6 minutes time verified by student F.M. and then 11 minutes 16 seconds by student C.S.

Explain the plot of Great Expectations. 15:30 FM

Give five Spanish words used in the kitchen and their English meaning. 5p KL= 5 points verified by student with initials K.L.

Give the definition of a trapezoid and how to obtain its area. 5p HT, 8p KL

Explain five ways students gain good feelings in school. 5p LS

Name four stages in the life cycle of a large aquatic mammal. 4p PP

The answers to some of the questions above are specified in points and can be used as they are. Others with a lengthy timed answer can be broken into increments during questioning. The ten largest rivers divide into comments about each river or can be chunked by continent. A questioner might ask first, "What are the names of the ten largest rivers?" and follow up with "Please tell all you know about the Nile." Five principles in geometry have five answers similarly separable. The question about American politics invites arbitrary division before the competition (cf. 6 below), perhaps by issues, people, motivations, cause and effect, events, or time lines. The contents of a novel might be segmented by beginning, middle, and end; or by events, themes, and characters.

5. *Total Team Challenge (TTC)*. The times and points of each one's Learning Feats are totaled to obtain their personal ILF score. The ILF scores of all team members added together are the Total Team Challenge (TTC), a list of the questions everyone can answer and the time or point scores of each. Parts of team members' lists are likely to be the same and others individualized. Progress from

practices shows up as an increasing TTC that the team can defend in the upcoming match.

6. *Long Answers.* The length of an answer affects both integration of the knowledge and the pace of the questioning, values that conflict. The competition is most spirited with answers that are brief and checkable, but we also want to build academic mastery with answers as long as possible, even explaining an entire subject.

   To combine both goals, divide answers longer than three minutes (the equivalent of twelve points) into two or more smaller answers. A student with an eight-minute answer might say "I'm going to answer in three parts," and names the parts, each of which becomes its own question if the questioner asks for it. A person with a twenty-minute answer might outline three or four major parts and chunk those further into portions less than three minutes long. **Accurate scoring depends on knowing the length of each part of a claimed answer.** The list given to the opposing team includes all the questions that have answers three minutes or under so each team can reasonably estimate what the other knows.

7. *Short Answers.* Ask students to express their answers in complete sentences. An exception to this could be straight memory material which by agreement of the organizers might have answers of a single word, phrase, or data bit. Even small pieces *that took independent effort to learn* deserve a point of score. Examples are spellings, times tables, formulas, definitions, and subject-related vocabulary (a point for each). For foreign language vocabulary, organizers can agree on the direction of translation. Early in the year they might work on passive understanding—the question in the foreign language and its translation in English (What does "hablar" mean?). Later when students have enlarged their passive vocabulary, you might reverse the direction, putting the question in English and its translation in the foreign language to challenge their active vocabulary (How do you say "to speak" in Spanish?). Organizers can compile lists of scientific and mathematical terms to include, or accept any text's glossary definitions as legitimate brief answers (cf. point 10 below). To bring both points and time into a single measure, convert them at the rate of four points to one minute (cf. 44. Score by Points and Time for more on how to do that). With these guidelines, long and short answers and both points and time can be included in the same overall score.

8. *The Five-Second Rule.* A superficial way to learn is to chop everything into answers as brief as possible. The five-second rule accounts for the information supplied by a question that makes

answering easier, and benefits the team that converts its questions instead into the most comprehensive arrangement. The rule treats as just one question any that a student can outline into chunks and the chunks into pieces that he or she can go into at any level asked. This encourages students to chunk up their learning and avoid multiple individual smaller questions that cost them a five-second time. Apply the rule by counting the total number of questions on the ILF lists of a team's members for which students can outline the answers completely, and multiply that number by five seconds. One on a team may have 60 questions with multiple parts to each (x 5 seconds = 300 seconds or 5 minutes), while another may have four times that many brief questions (240 questions x 5 seconds each = 20 minutes), and a third may know his or her entire ILF list, which waives the five-second rule. At the Checkout (below), each student brackets the question-chunks he/she claims to know so that this information is available to the opposing team at the Exchange (to become a legitimate focus of challenge during questioning) and is supplied to the judge.

FINAL PREPARATION

9. *The Checkout.* In the last practice session before the meet called "the checkout," students score Individual Learning Feats they want to claim that haven't been scored already. They add up their collective ILF scores to produce the Total Team Challenge (TTC), assemble in a package all the papers containing their questions that have claimed scores no longer than three minutes but without the answer details, and make a copy of it for the opposing team and the judge.

10. *The Exchange.* For the first meet, exchange lists an hour ahead and decide afterward if you want more or less time for future meets. An issue to settle is that each team accept the other's TTC as valid learning. To pad their record, a team might go to a dictionary and pick out a thousand common words they already know how to spell and claim an extra thousand points apiece for each member. Teams need to agree that the opposing team's material is valid for their grade level. If it isn't, they protest it to their teacher who either works it out with the opposing team or they present the issue to the judge for resolution (possibly adjusting the TTC lower) before the competition begins. Organizers avoid such problems by agreeing ahead about categories or sources of knowledge presumed acceptable. A second issue is that the lists of questions exchanged must be readily legible and neatly organized so they don't slow the questioning process.

11. *The Strategy Session.* In the time between the Exchange and the Meet, with the opposing team's valid TTC in hand, team members study it to select the Learning Feats on it that they believe give them the best edge in questioning; where they believe opponents are most vulnerable and their own knowledge can best help them expose it. They also might wish to scramble after sources on ideas they're not familiar with. They prepare a list of questions to address to each individual opponent that anyone on their own team can use when named questioner. They might also note from the opposing team's list that they can expect intense questioning themselves on specific subjects and decide to refresh their knowledge about them. Teams may need less than an hour to do this, so the meet can begin anytime both teams are ready.

12. *Risk/Reward.* The beginning TTC is the basis of the team's score. The scoring system rewards the team that risks the most, that declares the maximum knowledge they think they can defend. The higher the initial TTC, the better the chance of winning. Yet including shaky knowledge invites the other team to expose it and gain points for itself. If the TTC scores are close at the start of the meet, the team best prepared to challenge the opposing team's answers with probing questions and defend its own answers does the best. The possibility that any Learning Feat may be challenged is a motive for mastering each one.

THE MEET

13. *The Setting.* Places are arranged for the two students who will exchange questions and answers. They sit facing each other at opposite ends of a long table or at small tables several feet apart, a distance enabling teams to whisper among themselves without being overheard *when their team is the questioner.* The judge is seated to the side midway between the two teams, receives a list of the members of each team with two columns beside their names headed "Point Student" and "Questioner," and checks them off as they fulfill these roles.

14. *The Questioning.* A coin toss determines which team answers first. The judge randomly draws the name of the point student (e.g. Joe), and the opposing questioner (e.g. Sharon). The point student gives his/her questions and answers to the judge. The judge or scoring team keeps time with an automatic timer that beeps when time is up. The questioning turn is five minutes for six-person teams, six minutes for four-person teams, or of a length agreed on by the organizers (who are free to try out any rule modifications they wish). Sharon asks questions that challenge the knowledge Joe

claimed on his ILF list. Others on her team can relay questions to her verbally or in writing to ask Joe but she, as the assigned questioner, determines which to ask. This guideline helps the team whose members have most thoroughly exchanged everything they know beforehand instead of relying on a few expert members. Also, a team that interrupts questioning to confer about a tack to take loses time for challenging the point student.

Sharon continues to question Joe for the time allotted on any legitimate part of a Learning Feat he claims to know. If his ILF list cites many minutes of knowledge about the Bill of Rights, he should be able to describe what the First Amendment can mean for a citizen. Joe may answer correctly, be wrong, be vague and unclear, repeat himself, or show insightful understanding. He answers to the limit of his five- or six-minute time while the judge consults his answer pages to verify that his answers are appropriate for the knowledge he claims. If Joe regards a question as outside his claimed knowledge, he can answer, "That question isn't on my list." If the questioner disagrees about this, the issue is left to the judge to weigh along with the student's overall performance.

Sharon can end any of Joe's answers by saying "Thank you" when she thinks he's revealed the extent of his knowledge, and ask another question. If she and her team suspect that he can't answer for a score he claims, they can make a tactical decision to ask him to tell all of that answer, or may presume that the judge notices the lack and try to find other weak knowledge. Joe can answer, "I don't know that one," and hope that with the next question he can demonstrate more mastery.

A team questioned may realize that they've just given answers they'd planned to ask of the other team, making it easier for the other team to respond. Their mastery shows up then as they can shift quickly to a different tack.

Questioning alternates from one team to the other. The judge draws two more names and allows the two who just competed to rest for a turn unless they're the last to be named from their team.

15. *Completeness Criteria.* The following criteria can help a judge decide whether to take points from the answering team and award them to the questioning team:

1) Speed. If the point student talks at less than a normal rate of speed, subtract the degree of slowness as a percentage compared to normal talking speed.

2) Padding. Does the student supply information appropriate for a lower grade that entailed no learning effort? Direct experience

should be combined with academic learning. A question on geology isn't answered adequately by telling about a vacation in a national park ("The mountains were really big . . .").

3) Repetition. Occasional restatement is normal, but for a pattern of repetition, subtract the proportion of repeated time from the student's total score.

4) Deficit. Was something omitted that reasonably should have been part of the claimed answer? Check for obvious gaps in the outline submitted and the answer given.

5) Inaccuracy. Was something declared true that isn't so?

6) Illogicality. Did the point student connect ideas inappropriately, showing a lack of understanding?

7) Integration. Judges can award extra points to balance off those lost (or even increase an ILF score) as students link ideas flexibly and insightfully, add more knowledge than claimed, and synthesize information. Aggressive questioning usually reveals the degree of integration achieved.

JUDGING

16. *Judges.* The judge's fairness in crediting individuals' knowledge, applying their standard consistently to everyone, is essential to a good competition. They do so by comparing a student's actual answer to his claimed answer for each question and assigning it a percentage. If stage fright disables any students from taking their turn, organizers can agree on a second chance after others are questioned.

Judges may be anyone from the school or community but preferably those who are familiar with the students' foundation of knowledge. Enlist older students if you can. More than one judge may be used and their tallies averaged. Don't schedule parents to judge their own children, since other participants will question their objectivity. Judges can meet ahead to learn the process and scoring. They assume a role similar to that of a referee in a sports contest to settle disagreements about rules that haven't been resolved already by the organizers.

17. *Scoring.* Judges use the Individual Match Worksheet to score each student. Immediately after each individual question and answer, the judge assigns a percent of validity to it, a conclusion about Joe's mastery using the seven criteria described above, focusing just on what he/she hears that demonstrates learning on the ILF items questioned. The overall proportion of mastery of the questions answered is applied to the student's total score. If the judge awards 90% validity to Joe's knowledge on the items *questioned*, 10% of

his total score *claimed* is transferred to the other team. If Joe began with a net ILF score of 2,000 points, 200 points are awarded to the other team and Joe's score is reduced to 1800. If his team's TTC posted on the scoreboard at the start was 10,000, it's reduced on the scoreboard to 9,800 and the opposing team's TTC is increased by 200 points. The judge can award the other team as much of Joe's score as he/she deems fair: 1%, 10%, or even 100% if Joe knows nothing that he claimed to know. If the point student responds perfectly on the questions *asked* (which may be a twentieth of his list), 100% credit is given for his total *claimed* score.

A scoring team can speed the scoring process. After entering a percent of validity for each separate question, the judge hands the worksheet to the scoring team which completes the calculations on it during the next round. So as not to distract questioning, it posts the results on the scoreboard between rounds, maintaining a running tally of each team's total. Scores (changing the TTC up or down) occur when a point student has less than or more than the complete knowledge about the question he/she claimed to know (cf. Individual Match Worksheet, Appendix 10, for detailed instructions).

The winning team has the highest team score after all questioning and judging are completed and points exchanged.

18. *Outcomes*. Between meets, students might plot their team accomplishments on separate line charts (dates across the top and the scores up the side) for the following values:

1) Initial TTC going into each meet.

2) Meet Scores, the team's total score after changes from the questioning are included. If this line is above or below the prior one, you might discuss the solidity of the learning they claim, or congratulate them on their skill in questioning opposing teams.

3) Improvement. This is the difference between a team's scores that concluded the previous and current meets. The team with the biggest gain from one to the next wins the Improvement Contest. Even if they don't win the meet, scoring well on the Improvement Contest boosts a team's self-image.

4) Win/Loss Championship. This counts wins and losses for all meets during a season. The team with the most wins by the end of the season is the school champion.

5) High Score Championship. The team that knows the most at the end of the season has the high score, determined by the highest of the final TTCs of all the teams in one school or grade

(after points are subtracted in the competition). A team that starts slowly can accelerate through the year and still become school champion by this measure.

19. *Inter-School Silver Bullet Meets.* Bringing entire grades from one school to another for a meet might be logistically daunting, but it's possible to include everyone in the energy of the meet. Begin with an intramural league in each school that incorporates everyone on sixty teams, for example. For a trip to another school that can accommodate eighteen, all sixty prepare expecting to represent the school, and the day before the meet the eighteen participating are drawn.

At the meet site, match teams either by random draw, or schools with prior intra-school leagues and records of team wins and losses can bring together their ranked teams if they prefer: top against top, second against second, and so on. If one school arrives with fewer teams than the other, the larger draws a random number equal to the smaller school's.

The winning school of the meet is determined by the number of its competing teams winning. With eighteen teams from each school, one with ten or more winners is the Meet Champion. With equal numbers of winning teams, judges can declare a draw or break the tie by calculating the sum of the total final scores of the competing teams.

Schools can compete in overall *school* learning (whether teams went to the meet or not) by two measures. One is the All-School Combined Score (ACS) for schools of similar size. This compares the total scores of all of both schools' teams. To calculate this, competing teams obtain their final verified TTC *without adding to it the competition points* they might gain from the other team. If they lose points during the match (making their verified TTC lower than their initial), the average percentage of that loss among all their competing teams is applied to all their non-competing teams also. Competing teams together losing five percent by judges' ratings lower the scores of the non-competing teams also by that percent. When these adjustments are made to a school's team scores, the total of all of them represents an adjusted TTC for that school. Between schools, the higher adjusted TTC total identifies the winner. A harder working smaller school can readily outscore a larger one.

A second measure equalizes size differences and compares their learning achievement fairly regardless of how many students attend each school. The All-School Combined Score (ACS) is divided by the number of students enrolled in the school or participating grade to obtain the *average* student TTC score, which is called the "All-School Individual Score" (AIS). In both of these measures, every student's score adds up, so students are likely to say, "We want to win the all-school titles. Come on, let's help you!"

CHAPTER 9

Pilot Program

After my presentation to the staff of Seattle's African American Academy, I offered my services free of charge. There was a pause.

"I'd like to point out," said the principal, Dr. Joe Drake, "that the price is right."

When the meeting adjourned, Leonard Dawson Jr., a fourth grade teacher, caught me. "When can you come to my classroom?" he asked, and explained his situation. He felt confident, he said, of his ability to get academics across and believed he was a good teacher. The problem lay in the students' attitude. The teacher before him had been unable to keep order and the students had "run her off."

"They were hostile and aggressive to her and each other," he said, and described several unhappy incidents. "They don't understand how to get along," he continued. "They fight a lot and they make really hurtful comments. Someone might say 'If you look at me again like that, I'll kill you,' *and they mean it*. By the force of my effort, I'm able to keep order and make some headway in learning. But the minute I let up, things just disintegrate."

The next morning, his students eyed me suspiciously.

"Doctor Jensen is here to help us learn how to get along better," Mr. Dawson told them. "Would you please give us your attention?"

We began with a simple exercise of naming a feeling. He called on each student and asked, "What are you feeling today? Can you give just one word about what you're feeling?" A brief but personal word from everyone was the easiest way to get their attention and to hint that the focus would be on them.

He went around the room addressing all twenty-six students and hearing from each one willing to talk; and then around a second time inviting them to tell what specifically gave them the feeling. They cooperated in a guarded manner with one-word answers. Then we began a remembering exercise, dividing the group into pairs and selecting a topic together. We asked the speakers to talk for two minutes and then for listeners to summarize as much as they could remember. On a wall chart we posted by each one's name the amount of time the listeners were able to summarize.

These were easy activities for entry. Each contained an assured success, drew on what students habitually do anyway—tell what they think and feel, and remember what others say—and enlisted those processes for an academic purpose.

Classroom order. Order in the classroom was a challenge, so the second day we introduced a new way to obtain it.

"This morning I'd like to do something different with you," I said. "We'll be starting and stopping a lot, so I need to agree with you on a signal to use to end what you're doing so that everyone stops at the same time. Otherwise it won't work. We'd use too much time going back and forth. So what would be a good signal? Should I just say 'Stop' or would it work better to say 'Class'?" They considered this in silence, so I continued.

"If I say 'Class!' loud enough would everyone stop?" I asked. Their continued silence signaled, I felt, a collective decision they were making whether to cooperate with me or not, and to agree to anything at all that limited them. They looked at me warily.

"Or how about if I clap my hands? Is that better? What would be a good signal to get your attention?" My questions communicated my expectation that we would focus their attention. Asking them to help me select a signal conveyed three presumptions I wanted to leave unargued that 1) their activity would have a pattern, 2) everyone would participate, and 3) we would use an efficient signal. The nature of the signal was incidental but helping to choose it gave them a sense of ownership and an impression of an orderly activity to come.

"Say 'Shut up!'" one student finally said.

"How about a word like 'Philadelphia'?" another suggested.

"I'd like to just try saying 'Class,'" I said, "and then if something more is needed, I'll clap my hands. And if that doesn't work, we'll try something else. So what I'd like you to do is to go ahead and talk for a half minute and we'll try it out, okay?" I looked up at the clock while they began talking. The volume soon increased.

"Class!" I said, and began counting seconds silently. Soon the noise decreased. "That took seven seconds and everyone was quiet," I said. "Maybe we can just use that. That was great! Do you get the idea? We'll practice it some more. It's actually fun to stop in mid-sentence because when you do that you know you've really got control of yourself and you can remember what you were saying. Then when I say 'Please continue,' you can start right in the middle of the sentence where you left off, and go on. If you're in a small group, people will say 'You were the one talking'" and you can go right on from where you were. Let's try it again. Go on and talk for a while." The noise built again.

"Class!" I said, and counted seconds. "Three seconds! All right! Far out! Okay, now try it again."

"Did we break our record?" a student asked.

"You're setting a record every time now," I answered. "Go on and do it some more." This time they were so keyed to the process that they found it hard to say anything and began other noises like thumping chairs and desks.

"Class!" I said, and then a moment later, "One second! Yay!" The class applauded for itself. I then explained the new activity, began it, and soon wanted their attention.

"Class!" I said. Noise continued. I looked at the second hand of the clock and began counting aloud: "Seven seconds, eight seconds, nine seconds, ten seconds, eleven seconds . . .". Finally there was silence. "Okay," I said, "that took eleven seconds, not too bad." Looks of pleasure appeared on some faces, that in a real situation they'd applied the rule they'd agreed on.

Mr. Dawson then introduced a new rule. He would give them a five second cushion of time after he said "Class" in which they could finish their sentence and return to their seats if they were away from them. After five seconds he'd begin counting. For all the time accumulated through the morning, the entire class would stay that long in silence past when they normally would go out for recess or lunch. The same method worked to maintain attention as noise arose during an activity. Mr. Dawson would raise his hand to indicate that they were accumulating more time to stay after their customary release. This was usually enough motivation for them to quiet each other when he said "Class!" Often they were totally silent in one or two seconds.

Dr. Jensen's mess. In the next several days we began to ask them to explain to each other more points of knowledge in the academic subjects they were studying. They enjoyed calling these Learning Feats. As Mr. Dawson extended this to more of his presentations, students realized they actually knew answers and could express them, and their sense of success slowly increased their optimism about learning.

Our random assignment of pairs for learning practice stressed some students by putting them with others they didn't like. One boy refused to cooperate with the girl sitting next to him. Guessing that even a tiny motive might tilt his attitude, I caught up with him at the water fountain.

"Look," I said, "I'll give you fifty cents if you'll pair up with her." A startled look came over his face, he thought a moment, and nodded. I drew two quarters from my pocket and gave them to him. He returned to his seat and from then on cooperated.

One boy interrupted constantly till one day I called him to where I was sitting, and drew him up onto my lap. He sat still and looked up at me, his feet swinging off the floor, while I pretended that he was a first grader to whom I needed to give extremely explicit, patient directions about his interruptions. From that point, he changed. Yet even with many small improvements, students often were inattentive, and Mr. Dawson in frustration would make critical remarks to the class as a whole.

When we discussed these situations, he realized that criticism was counter-productive and made an important shift. He approached students individually, eyeball to eyeball, said in a respectful tone of voice that he was disappointed in their behavior, and told them what he wanted them to do. Behaviors changed further. Even so, several activities we tried were beyond their skills and would degenerate into disorder. Toward the end of the first week, a student came to Mr. Dawson.

"Are we going to have that Dr. Jensen mess again?" he asked indignantly.

True feelings. An incident occurred in the second week that changed the quality of the classroom experience. From being artificial, guarded, and focused on external behavior, it became internal to them, occupying their emotions, shifting motivation from outer to inner.

As I observed that morning, Mr. Dawson asked each student in turn to give a single word that described his or her feeling right then. The fifth student he questioned was a boy slumped in his chair who answered in a low voice, "Sad."

After everyone had answered, Mr. Dawson began a second time with "What was it that gave you that feeling?" This time, the boy choked out, "My aunt died last night."

There was confusion and silence. All were stunned. Many had known his aunt and were closely attuned to each other's moods, but had no idea how to respond. Mr. Dawson expressed his own feelings of sadness, invited the boy to tell what had happened, and then asked others to share what they felt about what he had said.

Several offered comments of grief, sadness, and sympathy as they encountered this new zone. A couple were crying. The issue was emotionally potent but felt very unfinished. What occurred next was decisive, I believe, a watershed event. Mr. Dawson asked if others would like to tell an experience of their own with death or loss. Nearly everyone's life had been touched with something painful, and in the next half hour many shared stories while others listened closely. A profound softening of boundaries occurred. They realized that they were not as separate as their prior hostility had made them appear.

The death of the boy's aunt was a gift to the class, making it legitimate to talk frankly about heartfelt needs and feelings. They'd let themselves be touched genuinely, and we needed to help them sustain that opening by providing high quality attention to each other.

The experience suggested a strategy any teacher might hold in reserve for the right moment: Prepare to respond constructively to unexpected trauma or disaster by drawing out its social/emotional impact and learning. Incidents often occur during a school year that impact everyone and temporarily free constructive emotions from their secret restraints. The teacher can respectfully open a way for each to express the meaning of the event for them, and take the class into a new ground of awareness. Expressed in a setting of considerateness and relevance to the day's incident, their new feelings are a powerful reason for them to accept new learning about themselves and each other.

Communication skills. As I went in each day, we repeated familiar program elements and steadily added new ones. The Communication Skills Check Sheet (Appendix 9) was a staple to improve the quality of both their social contact and academic work. We divided them into discussion groups of three and four for eight minutes, asked them to check themselves on the CSCS, and then next time the student on their right. They cooperated readily, enjoyed rating themselves and each other, and became more receptive to working with different people. As they memorized the points on the CSCS, we plotted their progress visibly on a wall chart, and did the same with rules for remembering.

Appreciation time. A systematic practice that influenced the emotional atmosphere was the Appreciation Time Mr. Dawson led daily. The activity began haltingly, but the class soon insisted on it. He would call on them individually by name, they'd stand, and he'd ask each one the same question: "Can you name someone who's given you a good feeling?" They'd say a name and then sit down.

One day, several named five or six others; a couple, ten or twelve others, while everyone listened attentively. They'd played a team sport during lunch period and had many sources of good feelings. Two said, "Everyone in the class is my friend."

When everyone had responded to the question, I assumed they were done, but Mr. Dawson started around again, asking "Could you describe *one specific thing* someone did to give you a good feeling?" They answered with wide grins and rapt attention, even students who a couple weeks before had been isolated and withdrawn. From the attention students were giving it, I had the impression of deep hungers satisfied in this forty-five minute exercise.

From that point, playground disciplinary problems all but disappeared. The student who had complained about "Dr. Jensen's mess" came to the teacher again. "Mr. Dawson," he said, "we don't think this is Dr. Jensen's mess anymore."

Some individual changes were by unobtrusive self-management. One boy who hadn't been able to restrain his tendency to interrupt undertook giving himself a grade every fifteen minutes for how well he'd controlled himself that period, and gradually modified his behavior (cf. 17). A student rejected by others had previously retaliated with insulting comments, yet as his own mood and actions improved, he found acceptance in the group.

At the end of the second week, Mr. Dawson asked the students to write me a note about what, if anything, had changed for them as a result of our work in the class together. Each one noted an improvement of some kind. Here are five:

> **Before you came our classroom was a disaster. Now we've become a little better. But we still need a little bit more improvement. Mr. Dawson has gotten better too. He doesn't have to raise his voice any more.—Damiko**

> **I have noticed a change in the classroom. Now they don't talk out that much. They know how to control themselves better than before. I know how to control myself and my temper. You have done a lot for this class.—Aaron**

> **You have made me feel like I can learn about people I never knew about. And I thank you because the class is much better now.—Florence**

> **When you came our class started to listen more. We are glad you are helping us with our problems.—Jolenta**

> **We have changed. Even I have changed. If you didn't come to this class, we would never have changed. I like you very much.—Dominique**

Organization groups. To enable them to take more responsibility for their learning, Mr. Dawson and I organized the room into groups of four to six students. We began by asking them to list privately the names of others they felt they "could best learn from" and those they "would like to be with in a group." Collating their responses, we identified those named least (who therefore needed the most support), identified others they liked who could be a bridge into group acceptance, and assigned them together. Multiple nominations identified those most likely to be accepted as leaders.

The five captains we selected met with the teacher for training and talked out an agenda to introduce to their groups. They might help their group select a group name everyone liked, instruct their groups in learning activities the teacher initiated, report on the progress of their individual members, reinforce good communication skills of their group, help those who had problems with schoolwork, and design some of their own activities. Some groups were immediately successful at working together while others needed help. Some responsibilities were shifted, but soon cooperative energy was flowing in the small groups.

One day the Seattle Deputy Superintendent of Schools, Mona Bailey, came to visit. Mr. Dawson chose to demonstrate small group sharing along with self-rating on the Communication Skills Check Sheet. Ms. Bailey sat nearby and listened in on one of the groups. After it was completed, she spoke to the group's leader who happened to be near me.

"What's changed for you in the last couple weeks?" she asked.

"I used to go home and beat up on my little brother all the time, but I don't do that anymore," the boy said cheerfully. He was now helping his group keep on task with an energy that appeared to me to be natural leadership ability.

I hadn't visited for several days when the teacher called to tell me that the students wanted to show off some of the Learning Feats they had mastered. At the appointed time, he drew names at random from a sack. Students came two at a time to the middle of the room where two chairs faced each other. They took the seats and in turn asked each other a question drawn randomly from math, language arts and history. They handled their answers confidently and returned to their desks, clearly proud of themselves. Mr. Dawson told me that the specific feedback they'd obtained through measuring talking time on their learning tasks had created a sense of excitement, enabling them to compare how well each was doing. It was competitive, he observed, but not in a way that anyone felt put down. Rather, all seemed stimulated by it and worked harder.

After we'd worked together for a few weeks, the mood and activity in the classroom had changed significantly, and students welcomed me into the class with smiles and greetings whenever I came. One day one of the group leaders approached me during a break.

"Are you going to write a book about this?" he asked.

"Yes I am," I said, laughing.

"Will you put our names in it?" he asked, looking at me with an excited smile.

"I'd be glad to," I said, and herewith include their names: Brett Fashaw, Alexis Mitchell, Dominique Michael, Tameka Green, Ikenna Joku, Adjovi Casselle, Michael Ellis, Mateen Abdullah, Darrel Holman, Kiasha Thomas, Fredrika Fisher, Maxie Jamal, Jolenta Coleman, Edward Roy, Curtis Riggins, Ardess Ballard, Ira Thomas, Dural Thomas, Kelton Dorsey, Damiko White, Aaron Johnson, Niyah Shields, Mandalin Richardson, Florence Paige, and Tavia Hinton.

Beginner's mind. "I had to adopt a beginner's mind about this," Mr. Dawson said to me. For the approach to work, he had needed to change—his intentions, his manner of interacting with students, his classroom control, and his design of learning. He'd decided to be teachable. A new habit he felt was significant was catching each student privately every day to make a supportive or encouraging comment to them.

Yet changing the class had been easy. He'd tried my suggestions, we solved problems together, and students followed his direction willingly. Activities were successful and pleasant, and by the end of the school year, six weeks after our start, the room had been transformed.

The central learning for me was realizing the cumulative impact of several ways to express natural motivations that layered upon each other at different times of the day or week. The activities weren't just an extra spliced in occasionally but were the manner of doing their main work. What they assimilated first period about giving attention to each other they applied during their learning activity in second period. The third period's sharing of good feelings infected the mastery practice during fourth period, and so on.

So what did we have? Activities converged: understanding the subject, organizing it so it could be practiced, practicing it, scoring it, performing it to the class, improving communication skills, and addressing feelings. Students experienced a teacher's enthusiasm, establishing a verifiable goal of mastery, getting the answer under their control, the pleasure of talking about what they knew, being assessed as successful by a peer, having their achievement quantified precisely, becoming competent with explaining their knowledge, and having their scores posted for public recognition. Here were the main components of the Silver Bullet Easy Learning System.

CHAPTER 10

Implementation

To the young scientists of his country, Ivan Pavlov wrote, *A scientist must accustom himself to the gradual accumulation of knowledge.*

His use of the word "accustom" suggests that accumulating knowledge is not automatic but requires unremitting, willed energy against a human propensity to distraction and lethargy. In educating, we seek to accustom students to channel previously unfocused energy into lifetime learning. Even a system of slow accumulation would show impressive power. Let's say that on the average, a student takes a full fifteen minutes just to learn one worthy idea contained in a single sentence. He grasps something new, gives it coherent form, and saves it—a new idea every fifteen minutes, just four per hour. At this pace five hours a day, in a week he has a hundred ideas, in thirty-six weeks 3,600 ideas, and in twelve years 43,200 ideas.

It's not speed that's decisive. Even at turtle pace half that fast—two ideas per hour—he ends in twelve years with 21,600 ideas. What's critical is saving instead of forgetting. To be wildly successful, he need only retain ideas at a steady pace, which we can accomplish easily with him if we just don't permit his learning to evaporate.

A principle of education arises from the nature of reality: **Organize the lower so the higher can flow freely.** The higher is the universe of knowledge we want them to participate in by their own desire. The lower are physical behaviors of reading, speaking, listening, writing, and recalling ideas. Organizing the lower is the price of admission to the higher.

The basic effort must be theirs, but how you arrange it is crucial. Chunk your class hour to take as little time as possible for your part. A clue to the proportions needed came from an instructor during my military service many years ago. He said that by time studies and long experience, the Army had discovered that the best use of time in conveying a skill to recruits was 5% of it explaining, 10% demonstrating, and 85% practicing. Applying these ratios to a classroom hour, you'd spend about 7 minutes conveying knowledge, and students would take 43 minutes to practice it.

Do your part efficiently, presenting material or directing them to collect it. Insure that they understand it and define it in hard copy. When you write out concise answers on the board for them, they grasp what's important, increase their concentration, and gain a learning tool. When they can assemble answers independently, you can cease writing them out, but if some can't do this, your contribution in writing may determine their learning.

Your writing paces you as it steers their effort. You prioritize by deciding, "This point is *worth* writing out so they get it." If it's not important enough to you to write it out, why should it be worth their sustained labor to master it? Expecting them to learn more than you or they are willing to write out prompts a self-check, "How much of this will stick?" Writing the answers aligns you to their rhythms of absorbing knowledge, shifting you from an attitude of "I hope most of you get this" to *"I'm writing this down because I expect everyone to get it."*

With input and hard copy phases done, you outline what they're to do and then step aside so they can do it. They use the remainder of the period to elaborate and embed the material in their mind. They may tell it to each other, or shape it by researching, making notes while reading slowly, trading knowledge, or summarizing in writing. They may practice repetitions of problems such as in math, or rewrite previous work. Then on a subsequent day they can increase their fluency in explaining knowledge already well-organized and thought through.

If you lead much of the class time yourself, at least intersperse it with frequent intervals of a minute or two for them to output the material to each other or check their ongoing Peg List, so that they preserve key ideas. A criterion for selecting among methods is, *How many will expend how much effort at this?*

To **familiarize students** quickly with the learning system, repeat its main actions with simple content several times in a row. Prepare the scoreboard (cf. Appendix 7) for recording points by their names, and organize their notebooks (cf. 1). Write the boxed steps on the board, tell them the

1	Present
2	Questions and answers
3	Partner practice
4	Score
5	Report
6	Post

rounds will go quickly, and point to the steps as you proceed:

Round One. Allot 15 minutes and aim just for roughing in the sequence of steps.

1. Present a little information such as a Life Knowledge question with one or two points in the answer (cf. 26).
2. Write both Q and A on the board. Ask students to copy them in their notebooks on the pages you designate. This writing step is a decisive change for many students because it focuses them on a

specific answer they can practice for 100% mastery. Ask them to print their notes for legibility, shareability, and speed. The physical effort to create tidy, readable notes channels attention and is especially important for the less focused.

3. Assign partners. Let them choose someone nearby. Instruct them to ask each other the question and master the correct answer.

4. Ask them to count up the score the other achieved (e.g. one or two points), write their partner's score under the question in their partner's notebook, and add their own initials after it for verification. Walk around and look over their shoulders. Make sure everyone records question, answer, and score in the appropriate places.

5. Ask them to report on a small slip of paper. One partner writes out both of their names and scores, and the other delivers it to you.

6. Immediately post individual scores beside their names on the scoreboard.

Round Two. Again allot 15 minutes. With the steps familiar, they should go easily, allowing a little time for learning. Change partners, offer a question that has three to five points in the answer, and repeat the steps. The rules for Perfect Conversation (cf. 10) might serve. They master the answer by explaining it back and forth to a partner and report to you. You add their new score to the old one and post the combined total.

Round Three. Estimate 20 minutes for the last round. With both steps and learning occurring smoothly, repeat again with different partners and no more information than they can absorb in the same period. Three rounds are enough to clarify the map of the effort that obtains a positive score for them.

Before introducing new methods, consider gathering **baseline data** so you can say later, "Here's where we came from." Students are encouraged when they see measured progress, you'll be reinforced, and others curious about the approach will have something to judge by. A school demonstrating the design for a district may wish to employ a full spectrum of the measures below.

The first thing to measure is students' explicit knowledge. The Silver Bullet design is intended to increase knowledge *students not only remember but are sufficiently conscious of that they can call it up at will*—which implies a different kind of test than the usual.

Obtain a baseline of such knowledge by asking students without warning to write down all they know about the subject(s) you teach and without consulting any sources outside their own mind. When they've done so, they exchange papers with another student and all go through them together with you. Explain what represents a valid score in their answers, and clarify any uncertainties. Credit them with all their points of knowledge—the details, terms, steps, examples, and separate pieces of overview and structure that comprise points as explained in the Silver Bullet design. Compile each one's points into their own individual total. Then after a month or more of using the design, do the same thing, again without warning. Because the model produces explicitly remembered knowledge, you can expect a significant jump in their learning and express it as a percentage increase. They should remember everything they knew at the first test and almost all of what they've practiced since then.

You may also wish to administer standardized tests before the program begins and after it's operated for a year. The time interval needs to be longer because such tests are less likely to be designed around what your students explicitly master. Because they're learning assiduously, they're likely to do well anyway but the margin of misrepresentation will be wider. A longer time frame ameliorates more of the difference between what they study that they deserve credit for, and what they're tested on.

Besides increasing learning, the Silver Bullet design also changes attitudes that in turn change behavior. To find out, arrange with staff members to log in raw data from their area of responsibility: library checkouts showing interest in learning, changes in litter and graffiti that show respect for property (e.g. with countable measures like clean up hours or number of pieces of litter picked up, etc.), in-class disciplinary events, referrals to principal, suspensions, unsolicited parental praise, absences and tardiness for all reasons, illnesses reported to school nurse, thefts, return of lost items, reports of violence and their degree of severity, conversations solicited with staff, students choosing to continue class work outside class, and numbers of students identifying others as friendly or helpful. Collect such data, say, for a week before starting the Silver Bullet design. Continue doing so to watch progress, or just resume the measures after a couple months.

Group Change Strategy. Students grow best when teachers notice their next step and help them take it. This in turn requires understanding what their next step is, which becomes easier as teachers discuss students' progress among themselves. When activities and interventions are on target, even first graders can rapidly acquire skills in communication and emotional self-management that an adult could envy. As you design a format for your students, try to include 1) a few clear, observable guidelines, 2) a specific time in which to apply them, 3) accurate determination of results, and 4) recognition for success.

If you and your school's staff decide to undertake a change process, a few helpful points are 1) that it affects people strongly when they believe they can make a real difference, and 2) its importance (such as the impact on students' lives and how their success could help others) guides how much energy they'll put in. 3) The change should have a clear definition, specific objectives, and time frame. 4) People are more motivated when they account to each other, so arrange reports back to the group. 5) They learn by reflecting on what enables the group to succeed or causes it to fail. 6) As they appreciate each other and feel their contributions valued, they'll take more risks, and change to the extent that the group helps them think through the meaning of the experience for their lives and work. 7) Leaders' personal sacrifice and commitment give emotional meaning to everyone's efforts (30). People said of one effective principal, "He went around blotting up spilled feelings so no one would slip on them."

Who implements? Besides teachers, others can initiate features of the design. Parents can sponsor performances, organize Designated Listeners, listen daily to everything their children can explain without help, and encourage teachers to teach for mastery. Advisors of student organizations and coaches can introduce Appreciation Time, the vocabulary of feelings, and ratings of affective qualities of teams and groups. They can tally students' use of communication and conflict resolution skills, and give feedback on them. Civic organizations can help sponsor and organize Silver Bullet Team Competitions and other performances, and supply awards and certificates for performances. Principals, superintendents, boards of education, legislators, and governors can make fundamental changes: 1) Understand how the Learn and Lose System (cf. 6) makes schools a barrier to learning, 2) declare the long-term retention of all knowledge by all students the unifying instructional principle, 3) grasp what's written above for achieving that, and 4) take it into account in decision-making.

Teacher Checklist. Any half-dozen of the following practices can cause improvement, but for dramatic results in a couple weeks, do them all:

Classroom Order and Cooperation
1. **Do I help students organize their learning tools?**
2. **Do I maintain order with appropriate consequences?**
3. **Do I exert personal influence to obtain cooperation?**

Presentation
4. **Do I create interesting classes that manifest reality, truth, love, and wisdom?**
5. **Do I define the priorities I want students to master hour by hour?**
6. **Do I put key knowledge in question and answer form?**
7. **Do I pace the introduction of new material to their assimilation of prior material?**

Mastery
8. **Do I schedule enough practice for them to obtain new mastery daily?**
9. **Do I provide daily mental recall?**

10. **Do I space follow-up practice to insure long-term retention?**
Scoring
11. **Do I monitor students' accurate scoring of each other's mastered work?**
12. **Do I post their daily increment of new mastery?**
13. **Do I provide each a periodic Academic Mastery Report?**
Good Feelings
14. **Do I teach them how to manage their feelings?**
15. **Do I arrange for them to give each other good feelings?**
16. **Do the students and I master good communication skills?**
Performances
17. **Do I arrange performances of learning?**
18. **Do I arrange for them to share their learning with a designated listener?**

The National Problem. Speakers on education often say, "We need . . . ," and explain multiple ways to improve the system. A few years ago an urgent cry was "We need accountability!" and the No Child Left Behind Act applied that premise to U.S. education.

There are better and worse ways to obtain accountability. The present design offers micro-accountability in a manner that also stimulates students to be successful and feel connected to each other. The NCLB on the other hand could be described as applying consequences for matching its definitions of success and failure while omitting a key piece, the critical element of *method*. It applies pressure on schools instead to invent it for their own situation. Even with years of attempts at this and 1.1 million pieces of research to draw from in the ERIC files, spotty results suggest that *method* still eludes the system as a whole.

Together the pages above comprise a comment: "Give these methods a chance. Students will be successful and happy, and daily you'll track exactly what they know." Once everyone understands how to achieve results hourly with all students, the legislation can be dismissed as a period piece, a good try in a time of national concern.

APPENDICES

Appendix 1. Feelings List

adequate
affectionate
alert
alone
ambitious
angry
apathetic
apologetic
anxious
assured
awed
awkward
appreciated
bad
belonging
bored
concerned
contented
close
competent
controlling
dependence
desire for
attention
depressed
determined
disappointed
distant
down
edgy
embarrassed
empty

energetic
enthusiastic
ecstasy
envious
excited
fear
flowing
focused
free
friendly
frustrated
good
gratitude
grief
guilty
happy
hassled
hate
hope
helpless
hurt
inadequate
independent
indignant
insecure
inferior
involved
irritated
jealous
joyful
left out
lonely

lost
loved
loving
masterful
mistrusting
needed
neglected
neutral
non-involved
nostalgic
optimistic
pessimistic
possessive
powerful
proud
protective
put down
relaxed
rebellious
regretful
rejected
rejecting
relieved
remorse
resentful
respectful
responsible
sad
secure
self-blaming
self-conscious
serene

silly
shy
shame
"small" feeling
sorry for self
spaced out
stressed
stubborn
superior
threatened
temper
tired
tolerant
tranquil
troubled
trusting
uneasy
unneeded
unwanted
up
valuable
wanted
weak
weary
wilful
wonder
worried
worthless
wronged

Appendix 2. First Grade Topics

One first-grade class listed the following topics they would like to talk about:

animals	plants	swimming	Christmas
food	school rules	puppets	zoo
families	how to be good	world	jokes
cartoons	songs	things we learn	rhymes
video games	P.E.	music	alphabet
TV shows	centers in the room	homework	birds
games	fruits	helping at home	computers
dinosaurs	coloring books	recess	extinct animals
places to go	colors	fish	trees
mall	washing	fishing	insects
shopping	movies	hunting	sports
school	playing with friends	Halloween	sports players
favorite books	numbers	Mother's Day	authors
restaurants	camping	meats	ice cream
eating with family		teachers	class field trips
cleaning the school		parks	flowers

Appendix 3. Fourth Grade Topics

A fourth grade class listed the following topics they would like to talk about.

basketball	football	soccer	baseball
sportswear	Indians	gangs	weather
gas	money	volcano	girls
boys	cats	clothes	fighting
principal	trees	homework	tap dance
dentist	games	wolves	kickball
aliens	hair	wrestling	free time
bears	body	boxing	

Appendix 4. Issues for Middle and High School Students

when I was close to danger
when I wanted to be free
depending on others
accidents
pressure from parents
pressure from teachers
pressure from peers
family differences
being a parent
I'd like to be able to . . .
Giving and receiving compliments
having my own family
feelings parents give you
the future
feelings from girls
feelings from boys
being a male
being a female
being made fun of
racial discrimination
authority
feelings about how I look
being picked on
being on a team
resolutions I've made
troubles I've had
facing a fight
my parents' generation
feelings about sports
family relationships
speaking in class
drugs and alcohol
smoking
if I could . . .
how I would . . .
feelings from money
creating my own feelings
groups I've been in

groups I've been outside of
law
fighting
how I listen
loss I've experienced
fear of death
being around death
controlling myself
controlling others
being controlled
saying goodbye
being guessed about
guessing about others
liking someone
communicating when it's hard
experiences with power
experiences with truth
experiences with a neighbor
experiences with a friend
experiences with work
experiences with lying
how I finish what I start
organizing myself
mixed feelings about things
wishing for things
wondering what's real
knowing an opportunity
hiding feelings
what I think I need
discounts and putdowns
asking for help
being on my own
feelings different from others
what I like about me physically
pain

my experience being liked
my experience being disliked
what I'm good at
what gives me good feelings
what I want to be good at
a wild idea I had
what others may not like about me
having to lead
how my moods change
being looked at by others
getting poor grades
facing a teacher
facing a principal
performing
fear of not succeeding
wondering if I'm ready to graduate
things I'm not ready for
how I see myself in the future
when others encroach on me
when I encroach on others
promises to myself
promises to others
worries about being fat /thin
worries about my complexion/hair
worries about my clothes

Appendix 5. Advanced Topics

ability
acceptance
accusation
acquiring
advice
agreement
alcohol
ancestry
anger
animals
annoyances
approval
attention
beauty
begging
beginning
belief
books
boredom
brother
calmness
care
causation
certainty
chance
change
character
charity
cheerfulness
children
choice
cleanness-
cleverness-
clumsiness
command
complaint
concealment
confusion
congratulations
contempt

consensus
control
cooperation
courage
courtesy
cruelty
cure
dance
darkness
death
debt
deception
decision
defeat
defiance
departure
desertion
desire
destiny
difficulty
disagreement
disappointment
discovery
disobedience
disrespect
dissatisfaction
divorce
drama
drink
drugs
duty
ease
economy
elders
elegance
elimination
embarrassment
encroachment
enthusiasm
equality

evening
exaggeration
examination
excitement
exclusion
expectation
failure
fame
family
fashion
father
fatigue
fear
feeling
female
fighter
fine arts
follower
folly
food
foresight
forgetfulness
forgiveness
freedom
friend
future
ghost
giving
government
gratitude
greatness
greed
guilt
habit
hair
happiness
harm
hatred
head
health

heaven
height
hindsight
hitting
home
honesty
hope
humility
humiliation
ignorance
illegality
imagination
imitation
immorality
importance
imprisonment
inferiority
influence
insanity
insensitivity
institutions
intelligence
intuition
killing
kindness
land
law
leader
life
light
liking
loss
love
loyalty
luck
marriage
maturity
meddling
mementos
messes

milestone
miscalculations
misinterpretation
money
morality
morning
mother
motivation
mountain
mystery
names
naturalness
necessity-
neighbor
nervousness
nobility
obvious
offer
official
oldness
opening
opinion
opposition
ostentation
ownership
pain
passage
past
patriotism
payment
peace
perfection
permission
persuasion

pity
plan
playfulness
pleasure
possibility
power
poverty
prejudice
preparation
pressure
pretense
pride
privilege
privacy
.promise
protection
punishment
purpose
rank
receiving
rejection
relationship
relatives
relief
respect
rest
restraint
risk
roles
room
routine
rules
sale
sanity

school
scolding
seasons
selfishness
sensitiveness
sentimentality
service
severity
sex
similarity
simplicity
sister
size
sleep
slowness
sobriety
sociality
space
speed
spirituality
strength
stubbornness
stupidity
submission
success
suddenness
sufficiency
suggestion
suicide
superiority
support
surprise
taking
talk

taste
teaching
tendency
thought
threat
time
touch
travel
truth
unbelief
uncertainty
understanding
unfairness
uniformity
universe
unreal
unreasonableness
unselfishness
unusualness
value
vision
voice
war
warning
waste
weakness
will
wisdom
work
world
you

Appendix 6. Blank Chart

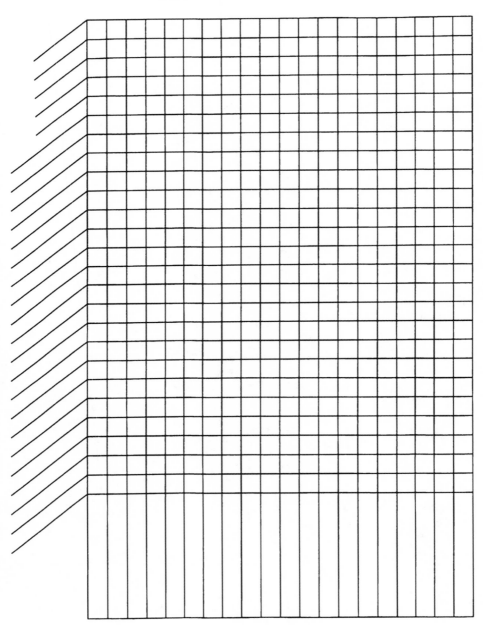

Appendix 7. Points and Mastery Scoreboards

Points Scoreboard

Name	Monday	Tuesday	Wednesday	Thursday	Friday	Cumulative

Mastery Scoreboard

Name	TIME Daily	TIME Total	POINTS Daily	POINTS Total	COMBINED TOTAL

Appendix 8. Progress Ladder

Progress Ladder	Date												
Each column is used for rating yourself on one day a week. Write the rating date at the top of the column. Draw a bar across the column at the level your progress reached in that rating period.													
Winners. Know what they want and act toward that steadily. They practice new habits and develop new skills constantly. They are willing to work at odd times, can sacrifice recreation for study or work. Will work at their goals while others play. Can face opposition and keep going steadily all day. Will work even when tired. Can face discouragement and get self "up" again. They feel valuable (able to create value), give others good feelings steadily, and enjoy drawing out others' best. Habitually considerate and acceptant toward all.													
Contenders. Some periodic enthusiasm gets person up and going. Can work hard but sometimes quits soon. Has goals but loses track of them frequently. Not willing to work when others play. Won't make sacrifices to achieve goals. Practices skills intermittently. Confident in some areas. Willing to be courteous, but only gives good feelings to those who return them. Lets circumstances become stronger than his/her own choices.													
Entrants. Is interested in doing better, but doesn't understand that this requires setting some things aside. Needs coaching and encouragement, but doesn't ask for it. Tends to drift. Will practice skills and develop knowledge if directed to do so, and will work while it's enjoyable. Depends on others to plan for him/her. Will help others when asked, but is more concerned with how others treat him/her than how he/she is treating others. Goals are more in the form of wishes.													
Undecided. The undecided is basically waiting, hoping something will turn up. The best he/she can do is wait in the presence of others who are doing better, and watch them, listen, look, and think. From this beginning, the undecided can learn to follow directions, and begin to think and work toward personal goals. Currently works only when inclined to, when there is nothing else to do. Is easily distracted by others and will set aside goals for TV, conversation, or old habits. Expects to succeed without any personal change. Is absorbed in own feelings and finds it difficult to give others sustained attention.													

Appendix 9. Communication Skills Check Sheet

Communication Skills Check Sheet	Each vertical column is for checking one experience. Go down one column (for example, column 1) and put in the rating on each skill for the person you observed:	0 = didn't use this one at all 1 = used it but poorly	2 = used it moderately well 3 = used it very well, or frequently, or very appropriately

Name _____	1	2	3	4	5	6	7	8	9	10	11	12	13
1. CHECK YOUR INNER ACTIVITY													
a. Notice others' desire to speak.													
b. Feel respect and consideration.													
c. Focus on the one speaking.													
d. Wait while the other finishes.													
e. Then share your ideas and feelings.													
2. LISTEN TO WHOEVER IS TALKING													
a. Look at speaker.													
b. Don't interrupt. Say "Excuse me" if you do.													
c. Ask speaker to continue.													
d. Leave brief silence when speaker ends.													
3. INCLUDE EVERYONE													
a. Invite those to talk who haven't.													
b. Give equal time talking.													
c. Ask questions and accept answers.													
f. Use others' names.													
4. GIVE A GOOD FEELING													
a. Take interest in what others say.													
b. Ask about their feelings and accept them.													
d. Thank people.													
e. Give compliments.													
f. Tell what helped you.													
5. CONNECT TO WHAT OTHERS SAY													
a. Remember what others say.													
b. Use others' words and ideas.													
c. Note similarity or differences compared to your ideas.													
d. Describe what affects you.													
e. Check guesses about others' thoughts and feelings.													
f. Summarize others' thoughts and feelings.													
g. Talk out problems.													
TOTAL SCORE													

Appendix 10. Individual Match Worksheet.

Meet location _____ Date_____ Judge _____
Point Student _____Team _____ Questioner _____ Team _____

1. Total mastery knowledge claimed by point student:_____

1	2	3	4	5
Question #	Time/Pts Claimed	Bonus% Added	Deficit% Taken	Time/Pts Verified
1				
2				
3				
4				
5				
6				
7				
8				
9				
10				
11				
12				
13				
14				
15				
16				
17				
19				
20				
Totals				

2. Question time credited (total of column 5) divided by question time claimed (total of column 2)= percent of mastery time credited _____
3. Total mastery knowledge claimed (line 1 above) _____ x percent mastery time credited (line 2 above) _____ = total mastered knowledge verified _____.
4. If line 1 is greater than line 3, then total mastery knowledge claimed (line 1) minus total mastery knowledge verified (line 3) = award to opposing team _____, subtracted from the score of the point student's team on scoreboard and added to opposing team's score.
5. If line 1 is smaller than line 3, then total mastery knowledge verified (line 3) minus total mastery knowledge claimed (line 1) = award to point student's team _____ and added to its score on scoreboard.

Worksheet Instructions

An individual match is a question-answer exchange between a point student and a questioner. A separate worksheet is made out for each individual match. A student's amount of claimed learning is judged during questioning to be stronger or weaker than claimed. If weaker, the increment is subtracted from his own team's total and added to the opposing team's; if stronger, it's added to his own team's. To determine this accurately, a judge weighs the student's claim question by question as the match proceeds. Afterward, the scoring team combines the judge's assessment of individual questions into a single percent that reflects the overall strength or weakness of the student's knowledge, and applies this to the knowledge claimed, adding the plus increment to the student's team score, or subtracting a minus increment from his team score and adding it to the other team's.

Students may score some of their knowledge as time and some as points. To make the scoring comparable for competition, organizers need to agree on which to use and then convert all scores to that one. In general, the younger the students, the more easily they'll use points and the older they are, the more likely time is preferred. The former are best for concrete, factual knowledge and the latter for synthesizing ideas. To convert points into time, divide the number of points by four (e.g. eight points divided by four = 2) and add the result to the total time (= add 2 minutes to time total). To go the other way and convert time into points, multiply minutes (with seconds expressed as a decimal) by four and add the result to the total points (e.g. 2 minutes and 30 seconds = 2.50 x 4 = 10 = add 10 points to the point total).

For rapid addition of times or their conversion to points, express seconds as the nearest quarter-minute so that each 15 seconds equals one point. Thus 1 minute and 20 seconds is closer to 1 minute and 15 than to 1 minute and 30, so as a decimal it's counted as a minute and a quarter, or 1.25 minutes, or 5 points. Thus 1:40 is closer to 1:45, so it equals 1.75 minutes or 7 points.

1. *Scoring team preparations.* The scoring team prepares for the competition and assists the judges and participants.

   a) They record on a scoreboard visible to everyone the initial Total Team Challenge (TTC) of each team. One design for it is a large dry erase board positioned vertically with a line down the middle. One team's TTC is entered at the top of one column and the other team's at the top of the other. As new scores are added and subtracted below it, spectators can follow the changes in scoring round by round.

   b) On the worksheet for each individual match, the scoring team enters the names of the judge, point student, questioner, and their team names; and on line 1 the amount of mastered knowledge the point student claims (as points or time, whichever is selected by the organizers). They hand the worksheet to the judge along with the point student's backup material when the judge is ready to begin the turn.

2. *Judge conducts the questioning.* The judge receives the worksheet for that turn from the scorers.

   a) When the participants are ready, the judge starts a timing device. The questioner locates the answer in the point student's material by giving a page and answer-number reference to the judge, and asks the first question of the point student.

   b) The judge records in column one the answer-number that identifies its location in the student's material, and in column two the time (or points) the student claims for it. He/she then listens to the point student's answer, comparing it to the answer the student claimed to know.

   c) When the student's answer for that question is complete, the judge determines whether the student actually knew more or less than the amount claimed. He/she assigns either a bonus or deficit, or validates the amount as claimed, and enters the result in columns to the right; a bonus in column three as a plus percent (eg. + 3%) or a deficit in column four as minus percent (-7%). If the judge validates that what was claimed was known, then he or she draws a line through columns three and four indicating to the scoring team that no adjustment was needed in the amount claimed.

   d) The point student answers as many questions as time allows and the judge fills in the first four columns for each question as appropriate. When that student's time is up, the judge completes the notations, hands the worksheet to the scoring team, and prepares for another individual match.

3. *Scoring team completes the scoring.* The scoring team receives worksheets for each round from the judge, completes them, and

converts the judge's ratings into an amount of increase or decrease of the team TTC score and records it on the scoreboard as follows:

a) For each question listed, they convert the judge's adjustment into a full percentage figure. If the judge gave a bonus of 3% for a particular question, they enter 103% in column three beside the judge's notation, and if the judge gave a deficit of 7% on another question, they enter a 93% figure in column four beside the judge's figure.

b) For each question, they then multiply the percentage figures (containing the bonus from column three or deficit from column four) times the score claimed for that question in column two, and record the result in column five for each question. They carry the multiplication out to two decimal places in order to register the difference between percentages assigned.

c) When all questions are scored individually, the scoring team obtains a total for column two and a total for column five. They divide the latter by the former to obtain the overall percent of all the questions validated or credited (compared to the amount claimed for those specific questions). They record the final percent on line two below the worksheet.

d) Next they compare this to the student's total, claimed body of knowledge. For this (following the blanks in line three), they multiply the total claimed knowledge from line one (first blank) times the percent entered on line two (second blank) to obtain the total verified knowledge and they record the product (third blank).

e) The scoring team determines the difference between the claimed score (line one) and the verified score (line three, last blank) obtained in the prior step. The smaller is subtracted from the larger.

f) If the verified score is lower than the claimed score (because of deficits assigned by the judge), the verified score is subtracted from the claimed score (line four). The difference is subtracted from his team's score on the scoreboard and added to the opposing team's score on the scoreboard.

g) If the verified score is the higher amount (because of bonuses awarded for questions by the judge), the scoring team subtracts the claimed score from the verified score. The difference is added to the point student's team score on the scoreboard (line five).

h) If the verified and claimed scores are the same (because the student successfully defended 100% mastery of his claimed knowledge) his or her team's score remains unchanged on the scoreboard.

REFERENCES

1. "Brain Imaging Identifies Best Memorization Strategies," Brenda Kirchhoff and Randy L. Buckner, *Science Daily,* August 10, 2006. Researchers at Washington University in St. Louis found that the memory strategies of visualizing carefully what was to be remembered, and constructing sentences about the objects to remember were the best of several attempted (citing the July 20, 2006 issue of *Neuron*).

2. "Testing Strengthens Recall Whether Something's on the Test or Not," *APA Press Release*, November 12, 2006. Researchers found that just taking a test helps students remember everything they learned. Summarizes "Retrieval-Induced Facilitation: Initially Nontested Material Can Benefit From Prior Testing of Related Material," Jason C. K. Chan, Kathleen B. McDermott, and Henry L. Roediger, *Journal of Experimental Psychology: General,* Vol 135, No. 4 (November 2006 issue). Authors note that this supports teachers' practice of regularly giving essay or short-answer exams that call up related or extraneous information: "This sort of all-inclusive retrieval strategy might be beneficial to retention in the long run."

3. *Pygmalion in the Classroom,* Robert Rosenthal and Lenore Jacobsen, Holt, Rinehart, and Winston: New York, 1968. This classic study illuminates the power of teacher belief. Many teachers actually preferred students staying as they were. Those labeled as poor learners got the most flack from teachers when they "stepped out of character" with improved results, even though it was the teachers' own grudging expectations that appeared to generate the results.

4. "Friendly Persuasion," James M. Kauffman et al., *Human Behavior,* September 1977.

5. If someone expresses a crudity about the word "feeling" when you start Appreciation Time, take it as an implied need. Ignore it at first, but if it's repeated, ask them "Are you uncomfortable with that word?" They may be, but try it anyway because it's the easiest to use: "We want to use words accurately, and that one tells what we mean, but if you need to, we can use a different one like, 'Who caused you to feel better?' or 'Who gave you a positive emotion?' Do you understand 'positive emotion'? Or we could say, 'Who was friendly to you?' Do you think

you'd be more comfortable with that?" Speak with a solicitous voice. You convey seriousness by insisting on using words accurately. An expert high school teacher I know focuses on the precise meaning of words to handle inappropriate comments from students. Before they ever begin, they know "I'm not going to get around this lady," and give up their distractive comments.

6. *Naikan: Gratitude, Grace, and the Japaneses Art of Self-Reflection*, Gregg Krech, Stone Bridge Press: Berkeley, 2002. Krech describes a philosophy of life and healing based on gratitude for all that's given us. Contains many exercises a teacher could readily apply to the classroom for stretching students' awareness and attitudes.

7. A discussion about how to describe a skill in either positive or negative terms may expand their understanding. On the Communication Skills Check Sheet, both forms are present; the affirmative in 1d and 1e, and the negative in 2b. From kindergarten on, children know the meaning of "Don't interrupt" because the negative form has been used so much more than the positive but discussing it in both forms generates better understanding.

8. This stripped-down set of five steps was developed in Alaska's Juneau/Douglas School District. Its brevity makes it handy for student use.

9. *Emotional Intelligence: Why it can matter more than IQ*, Daniel Goleman, Bantam Books: New York, 1995. Goleman devotes Chapter 6 to "The Master Aptitude," the ability to regulate our moods. The entire book explores different facets of emotional self-management. Its explanation of how emotion "hijacks" thinking could help many teachers.

10. Be aware of how your terminology translates to students. Most may understand that "bad" feelings are "unpleasant, sad, or unhappy," but some may code the term as "blameworthy." To make sure everyone understands your words in the same way, you may need to explain them when you first use them

11. *Health Dispatch*, Dr. David Williams, December 2003. Cites researchers at the Karolinska Hospital in Sweden who discovered that humming increases air exchange in the sinus cavities, helping them produce nitric oxide, which in turn helps dilate capillary beds and increase blood flow. During humming, nitric oxide levels appear to be 15 times higher than during normal breathing and the gas exchange between the nasal passages and the sinuses was 98 percent in one exhalation, almost a complete exchange whereas 4 percent is normal. This matters because poor gas exchange and circulation in the sinus cavities make bacterial growth and infection easier. Researchers feel that daily breathing

exercises involving humming could help reduce the incidence of sinusitis and upper respiratory infections. Done for long periods, this is likely to lead to increased mental clarity by increasing blood flow and oxygenation in the brain, and may alleviate chronic sinus problems. (Am J Respir Crit Care Med 02;166(2):131-2).

12 The concept of a resource state has been developed in numerous books by John Grinder and Richard Bandler as part of a therapeutic approach called Neuro-Linguistic Programming (NLP). Cf. *Trance-Formations* and *Frogs Into Princes,* both by John Grinder and Richard Bandler, Real People Press, Moab, Utah, 1979. Most development involves obtaining greater access to resource states or creating them where they're missing. The process described is a way to restore people to their personal strengths. Extensive applications of these ideas are available by searching "neuro-linguistic programming."

13. Said to be the basis of most civil law, these questions are taken from Richard Maybury, *Whatever Happened to Justice?*, Bluestocking Press: Shingle Springs, CA, 1990.

14. These two questions, a constructive stance to all interactions, are the basis of the ECK Neighbor Program.

15. "Optimization Versus Effortful Processing in Children: Cognitive Triage: Criticisms, Reanalyses, and New Data," C. J. Brainerd, et al *Journal of Experimental Child Psychology,* V55, N3, p353-73, June 1993.

16. *The Tipping Point: How Little Things Can Make a Big Difference,* Malcolm Gladwell, Little, Brown and Company: New York, 2000. Gladwell explains the psychology behind the Broken Windows theory, that correcting small misbehaviors diminishes the large misbehaviors that would occur otherwise. Its outcomes in New York City offer many parallels for how it can be applied to schools.

17. Classroom rules can be an occasion to discuss values and choices. Teachers in your school may have suggestions about what's worked with students like yours. One middle school teacher used the following that invites a thoughtful stance toward the system, physical objects, and people: 1) Do your best. 2) Don't interfere. Allow others to do their best. 3) Follow all lawful directives of staff the first time. 4) Don't divert the class. Solve problems outside class. 5) Respect private and public property. 6) Be considerate to all others in and outside of class.

18. "Cooperative Learning in Dyads," Celia O. Larson, *Journal of Reading,* V29, N6, p516-520, March 1986.

19. See reference 2.

20. See reference 1.

21. "Sleep to Remember," Matthew P. Walker, *American Scientist*, July-August 2006. Summarizes the forms of memory and how practice,

rehearsal and sleep relate. Sleep is important in consolidating memory, and adequate sleep is especially necessary to prepare the brain to receive and sustain new memory.

22. The three-step "universal success formula" proposed by Richard Bandler and John Grinder is a useful piece of knowledge to pass on to students: well-formed goals (so you have direction), sensory acuity (so you know whether you're getting there), and behavioral flexibility (so you can change what you do to get better results). See reference 12.

23. "Novelty Aids Learning," *Eurekalert*, August 3, 2006, summarizing an article published in *Neuron* August 3, 2006.

24. *What Smart Students Know: Maximum Grades, Optimum Learning, Minimum Time*, Adam Robinson, Random House: New York, 1993. Robinson explains why reorganizing and summarizing is a valuable means of retaining knowledge.

25. If you're a principal or trainer and would like to impress teachers with how they may unwittingly make students feel bad, give them a spelling test. Introduce it early on a training day by saying, "I'd like to assign people to the next exercises today based on how well you do on this first one, a college freshman spelling test." On a separate sheet of paper, have them write the following words (or a portion) as you dictate them with a straight face: asinine, braggadocio, accommodate, diarrhea, chauffeur, desiccate, impostor, inoculate, hors d'oeuvres, liquefy, mayonnaise, moccasin, obbligato, narcissistically, rococo, benefited, rarefy, resuscitate, sacrilegious, supersede, titillate, and paraphernalia. They exchange papers and you spell the words correctly while they place an X beside the wrong answers on the paper they have. They record the number wrong at the top and hand it back. Invite their results. List a column of numbers from zero down to twenty on the board. Ask "Who got none wrong?" Beside the 0, record the number—if any—who raise their hands, and proceed down the list asking the same question about each number: "Who got one wrong?" and so on. When all scores are noted, ask them how they feel. The exercise typically generates laughter but also reminds them of the viewpoint and feelings of children. In small groups, invite them to discuss how their experience with the spelling test might influence their instructional approach.

26. "Rutgers-Newark Researcher: Brains of Dyslexic Children can be 'Rewired' to Improve Reading Skills," *Rutgers-Newark News Service*, March 4, 2003, and "Dyslexics Not Doomed to Life of Reading Difficulties," Joel Schwarz, University of Washington, February 13, 2004. Studies from different sources are finding that teaching dyslexics by means of the links between sound, letters, and meaning can dramatically improve their reading.

27. If I'm a parent receiving my child's report and see an A, a B, and a C, what do they mean? I don't know because they're not linked to any stable reference point but rather reflect the teacher's comparison of him with those on either side of him. They often give a false picture, a B in one school may equal a D in another, grade inflation is endemic, grades can be assigned to pacify parents and not jar students, physical presence or verbal participation matter more to some teachers than to others, unconscious beliefs about status and racial bias can skew grades, tests for one demographic may be unfair to others, and teachers may want to "send a message." Courses in how to take tests distort the meaning of differences in scores, teaching to the test can cause an overall decrease in learning, and grading on the curve removes it from a direct relationship to the student's own effort.

28. For students raised under cultural norms that young people should remain silent, mention to them that a classroom differs from being in the presence of elders. All their lives they'll need to grasp the standards of the setting they're in ("When in Rome . . ."). In school, they develop knowledge by expressing it.

29. "How We Know: What Do an Algebra Teacher, Toyota, and a Classical Musician Have in Common?", Jonah Lehrer, *Seed*, September 2006, pp 70-73. Lehrer notes Ericsson's finding that peak performers practice differently than others. They do fewer mindless drills and less rote repetition but make sessions deliberate, creative and thoughtful. They set goals, analyze their progress steadily, and focus on their process of learning, always integrating learning with their doing.

30. "Film Shows How Teams Bring Out Best in People," Doug Wallace, *Minneapolis Star Tribune,* April 10, 1995, p2D.